August Nebe

Luther as Spiritual Adviser

August Nebe

Luther as Spiritual Adviser

ISBN/EAN: 9783337127299

Printed in Europe, USA, Canada, Australia, Japan

Cover: Foto ©Lupo / pixelio.de

More available books at **www.hansebooks.com**

LUTHER

AS

SPIRITUAL ADVISER.

AUGUST NEBE.

DOCTOR OF THEOLOGY, PROFESSOR, PASTOR.

TRANSLATED BY

CHARLES A. HAY, D. D.,
CHARLES E. HAY, A. M.

PHILADELPHIA:
LUTHERAN PUBLICATION SOCIETY.

TRANSLATOR'S PREFACE.

IT is hoped that the following presentation of the Leader of the Reformation as an untitled pastor, with all Germany for his parish, may not only serve to bring out into clearer view the wonderful versatility of the great man, and furnish a needed correction in the prevailing estimate of his character, but may also indicate to some a much-neglected field of Christian activity in our own age, an age in which temptations are varied in form and multiplied in power, and in which the occupants of pulpit and pew too often plead the pressure of official duties, absolutely trifling compared with those of Luther, as exempting from the primary obligations of Christian brotherhood.

The translation from the original has been, upon the part of the undersigned, a labor of filial love, the first pages having been prepared for the press by an honored father, Professor Charles A. Hay, D. D., of Gettysburg, Pa., but a few days before his summons to heavenly rest.

Thankful for the privilege of carrying out the design of one who himself exemplified in no small measure the true pastoral instinct, we commend this touching picture of the past to the contemplation of the present, imploring upon it the blessing of the great Shepherd of Souls.

CHARLES E. HAY.

ALLENTOWN, PA., JULY 2, 1894.

AUTHOR'S PREFACE.

ANOTHER small contribution to the quadri-centennial birthday banquet of Luther; we hope not an undesirable or superfluous one. That side of the Reformer's character which we try to present here dare not be merely glanced at, but deserves to be attentively considered. Here we may look down most deeply into his heart, for here the soul of his grand work reveals itself to us.

Constant reference has been made to the sources, and, where it was necessary, the Latin has been translated into German, as this little book is meant to be intelligible to everybody.

AUGUST NEBE.

ROSSLEBEN, SEPTEMBER, 1883.

"Bear ye one another's burdens, and so fulfil the law of Christ."—GAL. vi. 2.

CONTENTS.

	PAGE
TRANSLATOR'S PREFACE	3
AUTHOR'S PREFACE	5

CHAPTER I.
How Luther Cared for his own Soul 9

CHAPTER II.
How Luther Ministered to the Sick 31

CHAPTER III.
How Luther Interested Himself in the Forlorn . 57

CHAPTER IV.
How Luther Admonished the Erring 103

CHAPTER V.
How Luther Comforted the Mourning 137

CHAPTER VI.

How Luther Strengthened the Tempted 175

CHAPTER VII.

How Luther Dealt with the Dying 222

CHAPTER I.

HOW LUTHER CARED FOR HIS OWN SOUL.

AN old proverb says: "Physician, heal thyself" (Lk. iv. 23). We know very well that not every proverb is a true word; that, even if it contains a truth, still it does not hit the point in every case. Would the Lord have acted worthily of himself and in a manner well-pleasing to God, if he, despite his finding no faith among those of his own family, had done miracles in Nazareth, or if, in view of the scoffing assertion: "He helped others, let him help himself, if he be Christ, the chosen one of God" (Lk. xxiii. 35), he had torn out the nails from his hands and feet and had come down from the cross? But this old proverb is and remains ever true in regard to the pastoral care. No one can properly advise and care for another, unless he has before-hand advised and cared for himself. He who wishes to help others as a physician of souls, must himself first of all have conscientiously used the true remedy. Therefore Luther, as a Spiritual Adviser, had first to care for his own soul.

There has been only One upon earth who never needed any outside help, who found in the depths of his own pure, devout heart everything that he needed for the true life: and yet this One, our Redeemer, in the darkest hour of his life said to his three chosen apostles: "Remain here and watch with me!" (Matt. xxvi. 38). However high, too, the Reformer stands, he yet often received great benefit from the counsel of others. As long as he lived, he remembered with the heartiest gratitude especially two men, who comforted his poor soul when, in the monastery at Erfurt, it was torturing itself with sins for the most part imaginary, and despairing of the grace of God, and who led it to him who so kindly invites to himself the weary and heavy-laden.

An old, pious fellow-monk, whose name is unfortunately lost, to whom he told his agonies of conscience, pointed him to that principal article of faith, in which it is said: "I believe in a forgiveness of sins." He explained to him this article as meaning that we are not only in general to believe that some receive pardon, as even the devils believe that David and Peter were forgiven, but that God's command is that every one of us individually is to believe that his sins are forgiven.* "Son,

* Melanchthon's Vita Lutheri.

what are you doing?" said the venerable teacher to his pupil, who with many tears was deploring his temptations, "do you not know that the Lord has commanded us to hope?" "By this one word, 'commanded,'" confesses Luther in his commentary on Ps. li. 9,* "I was so strengthened that I knew that the absolution was to be believed. I had indeed often before heard the absolution, but, hindered by foolish thoughts, had supposed I dared not believe it, but heard it as if it did not avail for me."

The general vicar of the Augustinian monks, into whose order Luther had entered, the experienced Dr. Johann Staupitz, gave further aid. This pious, practical mystic had looked deeply into the heart of Holy Scripture, as well as into the human heart. "There is a great mountain. 'You must cross it'—the law says; 'I will cross it'—says presumption; 'You cannot'—says conscience; 'Then I won't attempt it'—says despair." † That was a word from him that Luther could never forget. Staupitz assured him that "Christ does not alarm, but comforts." "Why do you torment yourself with these speculations?", Staupitz once called to him.‡ "Look at the wounds of Christ and

---

* Op., ex. ed. Erlangen, 19, 100.
† Tischreden. Aurifaber, 149, b. Förstemann, 2, 48.
‡ Op. ex., 6, 296, on Gen. xxvi.

at his blood shed for you; from these predestination will shine forth." A casual remark of his, that only that repentance is genuine which begins with love to righteousness and to God,* remained, as Luther himself expresses it, sticking like the sharp arrow of a warrior in his soul, and he found the Scriptures to be in perfect harmony with it. Through his Staupitz, as he afterwards liked to call him, he was liberated from the morbid consciousness of sin by the statement: "You want to be an imaginary sinner and to regard Christ as an imaginary Saviour. You must accustom yourself to think that Christ is a real Saviour and that you are a real sinner. God does nothing for fun nor for show, and he is not joking when he sends his Son and delivers him up for us." † Often, when he came with his self-condemnatory complaints, he was dismissed with the answer: "Magister Martin, that I do not understand." ‡ "To Doctor Staupitz," thus Luther relates in his Tischreden,§ "I have often confessed, not about women, but real knotty questions, when he would reply: 'I don't understand it.' That was giving comfort rightly.

*Briefe. De Wette, 1, 116.
†Ibid., 5, 680.
‡Tischreden, Aurif., 314, b. Först., 3, 119.
§ Aurif., 320, a. Först., 3, 135.

At last Dr. Staupitz began with me as we were eating, and I was so sad and dejected, saying: 'Why are you so sad, brother Martin?' Then I said: 'O, what shall I do?' Said he: 'Ah, you do not know that this trial is good and necessary for you, else nothing good would ever come of you.' That he did not himself understand, for he thought I was learned, and if I had no temptations I should become proud and haughty. But I made the application in accordance with the saying of Paul: 'A thorn in the flesh was given to me, lest I should be exalted above measure.' Therefore I accepted it as a word uttered by the voice of the Holy Spirit."

Though Luther, already in the monastery, had made the experience that those of whom he hoped that they might understand his spiritual anxieties and sufferings could frequently not advise nor help him, this experience still did not prevent him from afterwards looking about for brotherly encouragement. He never regarded himself as all-sufficient, nor as highly lifted up above all others; humbly and urgently he besought help in hours of trial. "On Saturday Visitationis Mariae (July 9th, 1527)," reports Luther's most intimate friend in Wittenberg, the excellent Dr. Johann Bugenhagen,* "Dr. Martinus Lutherus, our dear father, had a

---

*Luther's Werke, Jena, 3, 403, b.

severe temptation, like those we are often told of in the Psalms. He had indeed previously endured several such temptations, but never any so severe as upon this occasion, as he confessed next day to Dr. Jonas, Dr. Christianus and myself, saying that it was much more severe and dangerous than the physical weakness which attacked him the same Saturday evening at five o'clock; although he afterwards asserted that even this bodily weakness had not been natural, but was perhaps the same sort of suffering that Paul had endured from Satan, who had buffeted him (2 Cor. xii. 7). When now this spiritual temptation on Saturday morning had passed away, the pious Job was concerned lest, if the hand of God should rest so heavily upon him again, he might not endure it. He had perhaps also an additional apprehension that our Lord Jesus Christ was about to call him home. He therefore sent his servant, Wolf, to me at eight o'clock in the morning, telling me to come to him in haste. As he said, 'in haste,' I was somewhat startled, but found the Doctor in his usual condition, standing by the side of his wife, as he was then able to commit and commend everything to God with a calm and collected mind. He is not accustomed to spread his affairs before men who cannot help him and whom he cannot benefit by his complaints; but he usually exhibits himself to people just as those wish to find him who come to him for comfort. If he is sometimes too merry at table, he does not himself enjoy it, and this cannot displease, much less scandalize, any really devout person; for he is an affable man, and utterly opposed to all sorts of dissimulation and hypocrisy. But, to proceed, I asked the Doctor why he had sent for me. He replied: 'Not for any bad purpose.' When now we had gone up and retired to a private apartment, he commended himself and all that he had with great earnestness to God, began to confess and to acknowledge his sin, the master desiring from his pupil comfort from the Word of God, as also an absolution and release from all his sins, exhorting me, too, to pray for him diligently, which I also asked him to do for me. Further, he desired that I would allow him on the following Sunday to receive the holy sacrament of the body and blood of Christ, for he hoped to be able on that Sunday to preach. He did not seem, so far as I could perceive, to anticipate the attack that befell him in the afternoon, and yet he added: If the Lord means to call me now, his will be done."

When, in the same year, 1527, the plague broke out in Wittenberg, and in the parsonage the wife of the chaplain, George Rörer, became a victim of it, Luther took Dr. Pommer into his house, "not so much" (as he himself writes to Nicholas Hausmann)* "on his account as on my own, that he may be a comfort to me in my loneliness." He joyfully acknowledges what consolation he experienced in the wonderful counsel of God through his guest at that time. "When, in the year 1535, the university of Wittenberg," he reports in the Tischreden,† "was transferred to Jena, on account of the frequent deaths, and I was deeply perplexed and sad about a certain matter, Dr. Pommer said to me: 'Our Lord God in Heaven no doubt is thinking: What more shall I do with this man? I have given him so many splendid great gifts, and yet he persists in doubting my grace.' These words were to me a grand, great comfort, and remained fixed in my heart, as if an angel from Heaven had spoken them to me, although at that time Dr. Pommer did not think that he was giving me a consolation with his words."

The Reformer desired not only the assistance of such prominent evangelical men as Bugenhagen and Jonas; he was glad, too, of the aid of the lowly brother. When, during the Diet of Augsburg in

---

* Briefe. De Wette, 3, 219.
† Aurif., 328 a. Först, 3, 159.

1530, he was sojourning in the castle at Coburg, he received every two weeks at the hands of the pastor residing there, Rev. Johann Grosche, the absolution and the holy sacrament. He extolled so highly to his pupil and associate, Veit Dietrich, the consoling instruction of this plain pastor, that the former begged Rev. Grosche to make a collection of the passages of Scripture that he generally used in absolution for the consoling of consciences. Grosche did this, and Luther, who afterwards saw the collection, was so much pleased with it, that he had it transcribed for his own use. For, in one's daily temptations, he declared, he had more than once learned in his own experience, how even the well-known passages often slip the memory and do not occur to one.*

That he cares best for his own soul who is completely immersed in the quickening and saving fountain of the Word of God, no one better knew than our Luther. We know what drove him into the monastery; he wanted to find rest for his soul. What did he first seek for there? "When I went into the monastery," he himself relates,† "I asked for a Bible and the brethren gave me one. It was bound in red leather. I made myself so thor-

---

* Porta, Pastorale Lutheri—Ausgabe von 1842, § 392.
† Ericeus, Sylvula. 174 b.

oughly familiar with it, that I knew on which page and at what place upon the page each passage stood. Had I kept it, I should have become a splendid *localis biblicus*. No other study pleased me like that of the Holy Scripture. I read in it diligently and imprinted it upon my memory. Often a single passage of weighty import occupied my thoughts the whole day. The significant words of the prophets, too, which I still very well remember, kept me thinking and thinking, although I could not comprehend them, e. g., as we read in Ezekiel: "I have no pleasure in the death of the wicked," etc.

The Reformer used the Scriptures for edification as long as he lived. God's Word was his daily food, and his unfailing weapon of offence and defence. Temptations often assailed him, not unfrequently taking the form of self-reproach for having published a doctrine of which the Catholic Church for a long while had no longer known anything, and of which in his day it would not admit an iota. Luther did not advance upon the track of a reformer with a flippant heart; he was too faithful a son of the Church that ejected him. "If the devil finds me idle," he says,* "and I am not mindful of the Word of God, he causes me con-

---
* Tischreden. Aurif., 12 a. Först., 1, 36.

scientious scruples, just as if I had not taught rightly, and had injured and distracted those in authority, and had been the occasion of so much scandal and disturbance by my doctrine. But if I lay hold of the Word of God, I am victorious, and can shield myself against the devil, saying: I know and am sure from the Word of God, that will not lie to me, that this doctrine is not mine, but that it is the doctrine of the Son of God. Then I defend myself further, by considering: What does God care for the whole world, if it were ever so great? He has established his Son as king; if the world will not acknowledge him, he has yet established him firmly enough in his kingdom, so that they will not unseat him, but must let him safely abide. But if the world undertakes to dethrone him, he will overwhelm them and reduce them to ashes. For God himself says: 'This my Son ye shall hear;' and in the second Psalm he says: 'Be wise now therefore, O ye kings: be instructed, ye judges of the earth. Serve the Lord with fear, and rejoice with trembling. Kiss the Son, lest he be angry, and ye perish from the way, for his wrath will soon be kindled.'"

God's Word afforded him perfect satisfaction. He declares:* "I want only the Word of God and

---

* Tischreden. Aurif., 11 b. Först., 1, 36.

do not ask for any miracle, nor desire any vision, nor will I believe an angel that teaches me anything different from the Word of God: I believe only the Word and works of God, for God's Word was sure from the beginning of the world, and has never missed, and I see in fact that things are going just as God's Word says."

That a perplexed mind does not find much counsel or comfort from the church fathers, he learned already in the monastery. Only Gerson, among the ecclesiastical writers, he praises, and even him only conditionally. "Gerson alone," he says,* "wrote hitherto about spiritual temptations; all the others felt only physical or carnal temptations: therefore also he alone can comfort and strengthen consciences, for he has learned it through experience. Yet he has not gone so far as to be able to give counsel to consciences in Christ through the Gospel; but he has made the pressing need or temptation tolerable and endurable by mitigating the law, saying: 'Ah, sin and death are after all not so very bad.'"

One good piece of advice from Gerson, however, he heeded, namely: "that one cannot in any way better avoid and drive away the temptations of the devil, and the thoughts that he inspires, than by

---

* Tischreden. Aurif., 310 a. Först., 3, 106.

just heartily despising him."* With all his heart the Reformer despised Satan, who tried to tempt him with all sorts of grievous and wicked thoughts. If he perceives that he is coming, he plays him, as he was fond of saying,† a merry trick. He begins to play on his lute and accompany it with a song. "One of the most beautiful and glorious gifts of God is music," says he.‡ "Satan is very hostile to it. With this one drives off many temptations and evil thoughts. The devil can't endure it." Or, he opens the window and looks at the birds. We know in what straits the Church was lying during the Diet at Augsburg, and with what serious thoughts of dying Luther was battling at Coburg, having even selected the place where he was to be buried. But how he threw out of the window everything that burdened his soul, and drew new inspiration and fresh courage from God's free creation! He comforts himself with what he sees, and is so consoled that he rouses up his friends in Augsburg‖ and Wittenberg with his exquisite mirth.

"Grace and Peace in Christ, my dear Friends!"

* Tischreden. Aurif., 322 b. Först., 3, 142.
† Ibid. Aurif., 311 a. Först., 3, 109.
‡ Ibid. Aurif., 577 b. Först., 4, 563.
‖ Briefe. De Wette, 4, 12 ff.

he writes to those at his home.* "I have received all your letters, and noted how matters are going with you. That you may know how we are getting along here, I inform you that we, namely, Magister Veit and Cyriacus and I, do not go to the diet at Augsburg; but we have been attending nevertheless another diet. There is a cluster of bushes just under our window, like a small forest. The rooks and crows have there assembled a diet, and there is such a coming and going, such a screaming day and night without ceasing, as if they were all drunk, roaring drunk: they are frolicking together, young and old, so that I sometimes wonder that their voice and breath hold out as they do. I would like to know whether there are any of these stylish fellows and restless trash still with you; seems to me they have gathered here from all over the world. I have not yet seen their emperor, but the dignified chaps and the lordly fellows are constantly hovering and bobbing up and down before our eyes; not very splendidly dressed, but all of one color, all alike black and all alike gray-eyed. They all sing the same song, yet with a charming variety of tones, of the young and old, the small and great. They don't care, either, for great palaces and halls; for their hall is

* Briefe. De Wette, 4, 7 ff.

arched over by the beautiful broad sky, their floor is nothing but field, checkered with pretty green shrubs, and the walls are as wide as the ends of the world. They do not concern themselves for horses and harness; they have feathered wheels, by which they can escape the rifles and get out of the way of danger. They are great, mighty lords; but what their conclusions are, I still do not know. But this much, however, I have learned from an interpreter—they are planning a powerful campaign and attack upon wheat, barley, oats, malt and all sorts of grain and corn, and many a one will here become a knight and perform great deeds. So we sit here in the diet, and listen and look on with great satisfaction, as the princes and lords, together with other estates of the empire, so cheerfully sing and enjoy themselves. But it affords us special pleasure to see how bravely they swing their tails, wipe their bills, break down the hedges, and prepare to gain a glorious victory over grain and malt. We wish them success in their pilfering—and would like to see them all together empaled upon a hedge-pole! But I think it is just like the Sophists and Papists, with their preaching and writing. These I must have all in a crowd before me, so that I may hear their agreeable voices and sermons, and see how very useful a people they are, to devour everything upon earth, and in return display their impudence by way of pastime. To-day we heard the first nightingale, for it distrusted the early part of April. We have had charming weather hitherto; it has not yet rained, except a little yesterday. Perhaps it is otherwise with you. God bless you. Be careful housekeepers.

"MARTINUS LUTHER, D."

From the Diet of the Malt-turks, April 28th, 1530.

But a look out of the window did not always suffice. Then in some other way a game had to be played upon the devil, who ever tries to make sad and desponding.*

"Dr. Martin Luther was at one time," we learn from the Tischreden,† "low-spirited and depressed, whereupon he was taken out for a carriage-ride through woods and across meadows. As his companions sang spiritual songs and were full of good cheer, he said: 'Our singing mortifies the devil

---

*The senior translator's work ends abruptly at this point, which happens to be the bottom of a page in the original. He here laid down his pen before retiring on the evening of Saturday, June 24th, 1893, and on the following Monday morning, after writing a few personal letters, he was gently called away from scenes of labor to his eternal rest.

†Aurif., 493 b. Först. 4, 252.

and gives him pain. But when he sees us grow impatient and hears us moaning, he laughs in his sleeve, for he delights to plague us, especially if we preach and confess Christ. And, since he is a prince of the world and our sworn enemy, and we must travel through his territory, he exacts tribute from us by thus vexing us with all manner of bodily sickness and complaints.'"

But, with all this, the devil cannot always be kept at a distance. He crowds upon one and begins to dispute. Then is just the time to play the wicked enemy a merry trick. "When the devil comes to me at night," says Luther in the Tischreden,* "to plague me, I give him this answer: 'Devil, I must sleep now, for it is God's commandment and appointment that we work by day and sleep at night.' If he now further persists, presses upon me and charges me as a sinner, then I ridicule him and say: 'Holy Satan, pray for me! Dear Devil, pray for me, for you have never done anything wrong. You alone are holy. Go before God, and gain grace for yourself. If you want to make me pious, I say to you: 'Physician, heal thyself.'"

The best weapon to employ against all trials and temptations is prayer; but Luther, great man of

* Aurif., 313 b. Först. 3, 116.

prayer that he was, experienced more than once to his sorrow that the spirit of prayer may forsake the believer. He understood, however, how to awaken it again and kindle it to a clear flame. "I am sometimes," he confesses,* "so cold and languid that I cannot pray; then I close my ears and say: 'I know that God is not far from me; therefore I must cry and call upon Him.' I recall, on the other hand, the ingratitude and the ungodly ways of the opposers, the Pope with his cankers and vermin, etc., until I grow warm and burn with wrath and hatred, and then I say: 'O Lord, hallowed be thy name, thy kingdom come, thy will be done.' Thus my prayer grows warm and becomes fervent."

By means of prayer he triumphed over all the sorrows of life and the terrors of death. In praying he attained resignation to the divine will, the blessed peace of trust in God. When, in 1527, that spiritual temptation and bodily weakness came upon him, from which he only very slowly recovered, he prayed, as Jonas relates,† as soon as he had regained consciousness after the swoon: "'My dearest God, if Thou wilt have it that this be the hour which Thou hast ordained

---

* Tischreden. Aurif., 315 a. Först., 3, 120.

† Luther's Werke. Jena 3, 404 a.

for me, thy gracious will be done!' He further prayed with great fervency of heart the Lord's Prayer and the entire sixth Psalm. When he was finally placed in bed, he began immediately again to pray, and said: 'Lord, my dearest God, O how gladly, as Thou knowest, would I have shed my blood for the sake of thy Word! But I am perhaps not worthy of such honor. Thy will be done! If Thou wilt have it so, I will gladly die; let but thy holy name be praised and glorified, whether by my life or by my death. But if it were possible, O God, I would gladly yet live, for the sake of thy pious and elect ones. Yet, if my hour is come, do as pleaseth Thee; Thou art a Lord over life and death! My dearest God, Thou hast thyself enlisted me in this cause. Thou knowest that it is thy Word and the truth. Exalt not thine enemies, and let them not rejoice and boastfully cry: "Where is now their God?" but glorify thy holy name to the dismay of the enemies of thy blessed, saving Word! My dearest Lord Jesus Christ, Thou hast graciously granted me the knowledge of thy holy name; Thou knowest that I believe on Thee with the Father and the Holy Spirit, one true God, and console myself that Thou art our Mediator and Saviour, who hast shed thy precious blood for us sinners. Support me in this hour, and comfort me with thy Holy Spirit!'"

The God of grace comforted him so richly in answer to his prayer, that he was able with cheerful confidence to bid farewell to wife and child. "My dearest Katie," said he,* "should our God at this time take me to himself, I beg you to be resigned to his gracious will. You are my lawful wife; be very sure of that, and have no doubt whatever about it. Let the blind, ungodly world say against this what it will; be guided by God's Word and hold fast to it, and you will have a sure, abiding consolation against the devil and all his slandering hosts."

Presently he began again to pray:† "O, my dear Lord Jesus Christ, who hast said: 'Ask, and ye shall receive; seek, and ye shall find; knock, and it shall be opened unto you,' according to this thy promise, give, Lord, to me asking, not gold nor silver, but a strong, firm faith; seeking, let me find, not worldly pleasure and joy, but comfort and refreshment through thy blessed, saving Word; knocking, open unto me. I desire nothing that the world counts great and high, for by such things I have not been made better by a handbreadth before Thee; but give me thy Holy Spirit, to enlighten my heart, to strengthen and comfort

---

* Luther's Werke. Jena, 3, 404 b.
† Ibid. Jena, 3, 405 a.

me in my distress and need, to keep me in true faith and trust upon thy grace until my end! Amen."

He then inquired for his little son: "But where is my dearest little Hans?" When the child was brought, it smiled upon him. This did not break the father's heart, but, filled with the spirit of willing submission, with the most cheerful confidence in God, he said: "O you good poor little child! I now commend my dearest Katie and thee, poor little orphan, to my dear, good God. You have nothing; but God, who is a father of the fatherless and a judge of the widows, will well provide and care for you."

The Lord at that time heard the prayers of his servant and of anxious friends, and restored him to health. When, at Eisleben, the dying-hour had really come, and he felt the cold death-dew upon his brow, he commended his spirit in prayer into the hands of God.* "O my Heavenly Father, the God and Father of our Lord Jesus Christ, Thou God of all comfort, I thank Thee, that Thou hast revealed to me thy dear Son, Jesus Christ, on whom I believe, whom I have preached and confessed, whom I have loved and praised, whom the miserable Pope and all the ungodly dishonor, persecute,

* Luther's Werke. Jena, 8, 385 b.

and blaspheme. I beseech Thee, my Lord Jesus Christ, let my soul be commended to Thee! O, Heavenly Father, although I must leave this body, and be snatched away from this life, yet I know assuredly, that I shall abide forever with Thee, and that no one shall snatch me out of thy hands."

In the days of health the Reformer had composed the noble Hymn of Simeon:

> "In peace and joy I now depart
>   At God's will,
> Within are cheerful mind and heart,
>   Placid and still:
> As God hath promise given,
> Death is but sleep to me."

Unremittingly, faithfully, had he cared for his own soul until the end, and the Lord, his God, therefore permitted him, when his hour was come, to depart in peace.

CHAPTER II.

HOW LUTHER MINISTERED TO THE SICK.

A MAN who has himself passed through severe attacks of sickness and temptation and has in this school of suffering experienced in his own heart the comfort of the divine Word and the power of prayer possesses every requisite which is of prime importance in ministering to the sick, and the only question is, whether he is also willing to do that for which the grace of God has qualified him. In this willingness the Reformer was never found wanting. He recognized fully and deeply the duty of the Christian man to minister to his brethren, to be the servant of all men in the power of love. That which he had in the very beginning of the Reformation set forth in bold outlines in the excellent pamphlet, "Of the Liberty of the Christian Man," he practically exemplified year by year in his intercourse with his fellow-men, and in times of need developed more fully and impressed with power upon the hearts of others.

When, in 1527, the pestilence not only broke out in Wittenberg, but spread, with devastating power, throughout all Germany, all who were at all able to escape fled from the infected regions, without stopping to think of their poor neighbors. Then Luther grasped his pen, and, at the request of the excellent Breslau pastor, Dr. Johann Hess, gave reply to the question: "Whether one may flee from death." This question he answers at large and in general in the negative, maintaining that only he can in God's name take refuge in flight, who is perfectly free and under no obligation, who has no special duties of any kind to perform toward his neighbor, and who is convinced that the general duty of care for the sick and the dead will be discharged by others. "For in this way," writes he,* "we must and are in duty bound to deal with our neighbor in all times of need and danger whatsoever. If his house is burning, love bids me run thither and help to put out the fire; if there are enough other people there to put it out, I may return home or remain there, as I please. If my neighbor falls into the water or into a pit, I must not go away, but must run up and help him all that I can; if there are others there helping him, then I am free. If I see him hungry or thirsty, I must not leave him, but give him food and drink, and not look upon the danger that I may thereby

---

*Werke. Jena, 3, 394 a. Compare Briefe. De Wette, 1, 347.

be made poor or less respectable. He who will not help and assist another until he can do it without danger or injury to his own person or property, will never help his neighbor, for that will always appear to him to involve a loss, danger, injury or neglect of his own interests. It is well understood that no one can live in the neighborhood of another without danger to his person, property, wife and child; for he must run the risk of a fire or other calamity reaching him from his neighbor's house, and ruining him with his body, property, wife, child and all that he has. If any one would not thus treat another, but would suffer his neighbor to lie in bodily distress and flee from him, he is before God a murderer, as St. John says in his epistle: 'He who loveth not his brother is a murderer;' and again: 'Whoso hath this world's goods and seeth his brother have need, how doth the love of God abide in him?' This is one of the very sins that God charges upon the city of Sodom, when he says through the prophet Ezekiel: 'Behold, this was the sin of thy sister Sodom, idleness, fullness and sufficiency, and no reaching out of the hand to the poor.' Therefore will Christ also at the last day condemn them as murderers, when he shall say: 'I was sick, and ye visited me not.' But if they shall be thus judged, who do not go to the poor and sick and offer them help, how will it go with those who yet further take from the poor what they have and lay all manner of inflictions upon them?"

No reproach could have rested upon the Reformer if he had removed with the university from Wittenberg to Jena. He held no office in the congregation, but was a member only of the academic body, and its chief member at that. The univerversity besought him to remain attached to it. The reigning prince, the Elector John, urged him in a special letter on the 10th of August,* to settle with his wife and child in Jena, as he could not be spared at the university there in view of what was daily occurring in matters of the divine Word and sacraments. But he remained inexorable, regarding it as his sacred duty to stay in Wittenberg and assist Bugenhagen in the sorely afflicted congregation, a decision which is the more highly to be applauded, as the first cases of death from pestilence —eighteen in number—all occurred in his immediate neighborhood, near the Elster gate.†

What did Luther then do during the pestilence? He himself tells us in the writing above referred to: "Whether one may flee from death." ‡ "I deem

---

* Burckhardt, Luther's Briefwechsel, s. 119.
† Briefe. De Wette, 3, 191.
‡ Werke. Jena, 3, 397 b.

it proper, therefore, to present at the same time some brief instruction as to how one should minister to the spiritual wants of the people in the midst of such frequent deaths, just as we have also done and daily do the same by word of mouth from the pulpit, in order that we, who are called to have the care of souls, may fulfil our office. In the first place, one should exhort the people to go to church and listen to the preaching, in order that they may learn the Word of God, which teaches how they ought to live and die. It should be kept in mind that those who are so rude and reckless as to despise God's Word when they are in health, should likewise be left to themselves in their sickness, unless they manifest sorrow and penitence with great earnestness, with tears and laments. For if any one chooses to live like a heathen or a dog, and shows no public sorrow for it, to him will we also not administer the sacrament, nor accept him as among the number of Christians; let him die as he has lived, and take heed to himself, for we are not to cast our pearls before swine, nor to give that which is holy unto the dogs. In the second place, the people should be exhorted that each one lay hold in time and prepare himself for death by confessing and receiving the sacrament once in every week or fortnight, that he become reconciled to his neighbor, and make his will, in order that, should the Lord call for him, and he be suddenly overtaken, before the pastor or chaplain can reach him, he may nevertheless have provided for his soul and not have neglected it, but commended it to God. In the third place, should any one desire to see the chaplain or pastor, the latter should be summoned or notified in time and at the beginning of the attack, before the disease has gained control, and while sense and reason still remain."

This instruction from the pulpit did not, of course, satisfy the godly man. When the pestilence then for the first time, and afterwards in 1535 and 1539, appeared and claimed its victims, he went out among the plague-stricken upon the streets and in the houses. He concerned himself most faithfully in their behalf, and did not hesitate to touch them, and to take them when dying in his arms that the last struggle might be less severe. Luther at one time spoke at table * of the death of Dr. Sebald and his wife, whom he had inspected, visited, lifted and handled in their sickness, and said that they both died more from anxiety than from the pestilence. To his beloved

---

*Aurif., 493 b. Först., 4, 251. Sebald Münsterer died in the night between the 25th and the 26th of October, 1539. Compare Briefe. De Wette, 5, 218.

Spalatin he writes on the 19th of August, 1527:*
"To-day we buried the wife of Tilo Dene (the burgomaster of Wittenberg), who yesterday died almost in my arms, and this was the first death in the central part of the city." He took the four orphaned children of Sebald into his own house, whereupon "some criticised him as tempting God. 'Yes,' said he, 'I had fine masters, who taught what it is to tempt God.' "†

But Luther was very far from tempting God: he does not disdain, indeed, in his little writing: "Whether one may flee from death," to recommend all kinds of measures against contagion. "Not so, my friend," cries he to him who says: "If God wishes to protect the city, He will surely do it without waiting for us to pour water on the fire,"‡ "that is poor reasoning; but use medicine, employ all means that can help you, fumigate house, yard and alleys, avoid also infected persons and places, when your neighbor does not need you or has recovered, and conduct yourself like one who would gladly help to put out a common fire.

* Briefe. De Wette, 3, 191. Compare Tischreden, Aurif., 276 a. Först., 2, 441.

† Tischreden. Aurif., 493 b. Först., 4, 251. Briefe, De Wette, 5, 219.

‡ Werke. Jena., 3, 396 b.

For what else is the pestilence but a fire, which devours not wood and straw, but the body and the life? This is the way you should reason: 'Well, the enemy has by God's decree sent in among us poison and deadly spawn. I will, therefore, implore God to be gracious to us and protect us. Afterwards, I will also fumigate, help to purify the air, give and take medicine, avoid infected places and persons where I am not needed, in order that I may not suffer harm myself, and, besides, poison and infect through my person many others and thus through my neglect be the occasion of their death.'"

Luther's own house did not entirely escape in 1527. On November 1st of that year he reports to his friend Amsdorf:* "It begins to look like a hospital at our house. Hannah, the wife of Augustinus (Schurf, a physician, whom Luther had taken into his home) had a touch of the prevailing disease, but is up again. Margaret Möchin (a woman from Mochau, who also lived with him) alarmed us with a suspicious boil and other symptoms, but she is recovering. I feel very much concerned about my Katie, who is in a delicate condition, for my little son has also been sick for three days, eats nothing and feels badly; they say it came from

* Briefe. De Wette, 3, 217.

teething." But God held a protecting hand over Luther and his family. That which he had written on the 19th of August to Spalatin:* "Only Pommer and I are therefore here with the chaplains; but Christ is here, so that we are not alone, and he will triumph in us over that old Serpent, the murderer of men, however sorely the latter may bruise his heel," was really experienced. "Thus we have," writes he in the letter to Amsdorf,† "fightings without and terrors within, and very severe at that; Christ is afflicting us. The only consolation that we have, with which to oppose the raging Satan, is this, that we at least have God's Word, to save the souls of believers, even if the devil does devour their bodies."

But not only in such very peculiarly trying times did the Reformer actively engage in extending temporal and spiritual aid to the sick. He always had a heart to feel for the sick, and through his whole life cheerfully ministered to their wants. He regarded the visits of the spiritual adviser just as much to be desired and as necessary as the visits of the physician, for he was thoroughly convinced that very many bodily diseases have their origin in a morbid spiritual condition. Upon one occasion,

*Briefe. De Wette, 3, 192.
† Ibid., 3, 217.

when he was informed of the weakness of a certain noted man, he said:* "That is a result of sorrow, which is often a cause of such disorders; for when the heart is troubled and sorrowful, then follows also weakness of the body. The diseases of the heart are the real diseases, such as sorrow, temptations, etc. I am a real Lazarus, thoroughly tried by sickness."

That no other spiritual condition can be created by the use of medicines, but that God's Word is the only means of help and healing, he also knew full well. "The physicians," said he once at table,† "consider in diseases only the *causas naturales*, whence and from what natural causes a disease comes, and try to give help with their medicine, and they do right; but they do not see that the devil often hurls a disease upon a person, when there are no *causas naturales*. There must therefore be a higher kind of medicine here, to ward off the devil's pestilence, namely, faith and prayer, and the seeking of spiritual remedies in God's Word. For this purpose, the 31st Psalm is, for example, very suitable, in which David says: 'My time is in thy hands.' This passage I have now in my sickness learned to understand, and will improve it in

---

* Tischreden. Aurif., 492 a. Först., 4, 246.
† Ibid. Aurif., 494 a. Först., 4, 253.

future editions of the Psalter. In the first translation I have applied it only to the hour of death; but I will make it read: 'My time is in thy hands—my whole life, all my days, all the hours and moments of my life; my health, my happiness, life and accident, sickness, death, sorrow—this is all in thy hand.'"

One of his household thus describes to us the method which Luther employed in his visits to the sick :* "When Dr. Martin Luther approached any sick person, whom he visited in time of bodily weakness, he conversed with him in a very friendly way, bent down over him and inquired in the first place about his sickness, what his ailment was, how long he had been weak, what physician he had employed, and what kind of medicine had been given him. Afterwards, he began to inquire whether in this bodily weakness he had been patient before God. When he had now learned, how the sick man had borne himself in his weakness, and what was his disposition towards God, if it appeared that he was determined to bear his sickness patiently, because it had been sent upon him by the gracious and fatherly will of God, and that he acknowledged himself to have well deserved this affliction by his sins, and was

* Tischreden. Aurif., 494 a. Först., 4, 254.

prepared to die willingly, if it should so please God; thereupon the Doctor began highly to praise such Christian resolution and purpose as a work wrought by the Holy Spirit, and declared with exultation that it is a great mercy of God when one attains in this life to the true knowledge of God and believes on Jesus Christ, our only Saviour, and can submit his will to the will of God. He then exhorted the sick to continue steadfast in such faith by the help of the Holy Spirit, and offered to pray diligently to God in his behalf. If upon this the sick began to thank the Doctor and to declare that they had not deserved to be visited by him, he was accustomed to reply that that was his office and his duty, and that they had no need to thank him for it. As he bade them farewell he kindly counseled them to fear nothing, reminding them that God was their gracious God and father, in confirmation of which he had given them good testimonials and seals in his Word and sacraments, and that, in order that we poor sinners might be delivered from the devil and from hell, the Son of God had willingly given Himself to death for us and reconciled us to God."

We are enabled, further, to follow Luther to several separate beds of sickness, and we do so gladly, because only thus will his method and manner become clearly perceptible. To the widow Felicitas, of Selmenitz, who had for his sake moved to Wittenberg and was there lying sick, he thus offered consolation.* "We have waited far too long, if we only now, in the last hour of need, would learn to know Christ. He has come to us in our baptism, and has been with us, and has kindly made a bridge for us, upon which we may cross from this life through death to the life beyond. This you must most firmly believe."

"At Torgau," we read in the Tischreden,† "he visited a chancery-clerk, a pious, industrious man, who lay sick with dropsy, comforted him, and counseled him not to let himself be troubled on account of this his sickness, nor to afflict himself yet further with sadness, but to follow the instructions of his physicians, in order that the blessing of God might not be hindered by anxiety and grief—for, as a common proverb has it, 'Good cheer is half the body,' i. e., if the heart is cheerful, the body will not suffer—and to follow the advice of St. Peter, and commend his soul to the faithful Creator. 'We ought to be glad to die,' said he, 'for we have had enough of life for ourselves; only we must live yet a while for the sake of others!'"

* Tischreden. Aurif., 331 a. Först., 3, 169.
† Aurif., 325 b. Först., 3, 152.

"Doctor Martin Luther," we learn again,* "visited and administered comfort to a woman, who had had a great longing to see him, but who suffered from a very grievous complaint and had passed through horrible paroxysms. No physician could give her counsel or help, for it was a pure work of the devil, an unnatural thing caused by terror at an apparition of the devil, who had assailed her in the form of a calf until she fainted away in a dead swoon. Several days afterward great terror and trembling came upon her, and she had four paroxysms, each lasting three or four hours, in which she fell prostrate upon the earth and fainted away, so that it was necessary to arouse her with cordials and cooling applications, and she became so very sick in consequence that she could hardly draw her breath. She would clasp her hands together, gaze steadily up towards heaven and sigh. Her hands and feet were so bowed by the cramp that they looked like horns, and were quite cold. Her tongue was parched and dry. Her whole body was even lifted quite up into the air and cast down again. In the midst of this terrible attack, she lifted up her eyes, which appeared as though heavy with sleep, and said: 'O, what a load I have had to bear! Take off this heavy

---

*Tischreden. Aurif., 322 b. f. Först., 3, 142 f.

stone!' As she was thus speaking, she saw Dr. Martin Luther standing before her bed. At this she was greatly rejoiced, sat up, welcomed him, and said: 'Ah! my dear Father in Christ, pray to God for me!' and fell back again upon the bed, saying: 'I am still so full of sleep.' Then said Dr. Martin Luther: 'Devil, may God command thee to let alone this, the creature and creation of his own divine hand,' and, turning to those who had come with him, he said: 'She is vexed in body by the devil, but her soul is blessed and will be preserved; therefore let us thank God and pray for her.' He then prayed aloud the Lord's Prayer, concluding finally with these words: 'Lord God, Heavenly Father, who hast commanded us and those who are sick to pray, we beseech Thee through Jesus Christ, thy dear Son, to deliver this thy handmaiden from her sickness and from the bonds of the devil! Wilt Thou not, in fatherly compassion, dear God, spare her soul, which Thou hast, together with her body, by the shedding of the blood of thy dear Son, Jesus Christ, purchased and saved from sin, death and the power of the devil?' To this the sick woman responded, 'Amen,' and then said to Dr. Luther: 'O, dear Father, pray to God for me, that I may continue in union with the Lord Christ, whom thou hast so faithfully preached to me, and who is my only comfort and my life; although he scourges now, he does it that I may become humble, but not that I may thereby be lost. But O, dear Lord Christ, give me patience and the knowledge of my sins!' Then Dr. Martin Luther comforted her with the Word of God, and said that she ought to acknowledge this paternal will of God and commend herself to him, for our Lord God is accustomed to scourge his dear children, in order that their spirits may be saved. The woman then made a noble confession of her faith, uttered a beautiful prayer of thanksgiving, and said: 'I have been proud and haughty; I have devoted more attention to the adornment of my body than to the hearing of God's Word; the preaching to which I have listened went in at one ear and out again at the other. But now I am in the right school, and God is preaching to me; therefore, dear Lord God, help for the sake of thy Son!' She gave utterance to many more such noble words, and said that when lying in the paroxysms she felt nothing and heard nothing, but only rested as though in a deep sleep and as though she were bearing a heavy burden, and that when consciousness returned she felt very tired in all her members. Upon the night following the visit of Dr. Martin Luther, she enjoyed a quiet rest.

Afterwards, however, the infirmity returned again, but she was at length graciously delivered from it."

The peculiar skill of the Reformer in ministering to the sick was known far and wide, and he was in consequence very frequently requested by such, if he could not visit them in person, at least to send to them counsel and consolation in writing. We present the three following, as specimens of the letters written in response to such requests.

To his old friend, the Mansfeld councilor, Johann Rühel, he writes :* "Grace and Peace in Christ, and with these, as ever, Life and Comfort. My dear and honored Doctor, my dear kind Sponsor and Relative. Your affliction occasions me the most heartfelt sorrow, especially as I have learned from the letter of your son Justus, that you find it so hard to bear. But surely you are, as well as we, a friend, member and confessor of that Man who says to us all through St. Paul (2 Cor. xii. 9): 'My strength is powerful in the weak.' It ought surely to make you much happier, to have been called by such a Man, endowed in addition with knowledge, desire and love for his Word, and, yet further, sealed with his baptism and sacrament. What more can he do, who has

---

*Briefe. De Wette, 4, 545 f.

given you within a heart thus disposed toward himself, and without such seals, together with the confession and testimony of his grace. O, dear Doctor, consider what blessings you have received from him, and look not upon your sufferings; for there is no comparison between the two. He can very easily, too, make you well again, if you will let him take his time: although we are his in every hour, as St. Paul says (Rom. xiv. 8): 'Living or dying, we are the Lord's (Domini sumus).' 'Yes,' truly 'Domini,' both in the possessive and in the nominative case: in the possessive case, 'the Lord's,' because we are his house, yes, his very members; in the nominative case, 'Lords,' because we rule over all things through faith, which, thanks be to God, is our victory, and tread upon the lions and dragons. Finally, remember that he has said (John xvi. 33): 'Be of good cheer, I have overcome the world.' Take courage, therefore, my dear and honored Doctor, and let the voices of your brethren reach your heart, through whom even beyond and above his daily works, God himself says to you: 'Where I am, there shall ye also be!' I shall treat your sons just as though they were my own. You are not a false friend to me, as I have had abundant reason to know: therefore will I also not be false to you nor to any of yours while

God grants me breath. Amen. Magister Philip will see you shortly, if God will, and will have more to say. I send greeting to all your family.

DR. MARTIN LUTHER."

Given this Day of Peter and Paul (June 29th), in the year 1534.

To the honorable and prudent Caspar Miller, chancellor at Mansfeld, his patron and sponsor, the Reformer sends this letter of comfort:* "Grace and Peace in Christ. My dear Sir and Sponsor, Honored Chancellor—to address you as is fitting, although some of those about you would have it otherwise—I have received your letter and the frills, which please me very well, and I thank you kindly. It grieves me, that sickness should again be laid upon you by God: for I know very well, since you are by the grace of God one of the very few (rare birds), who are heartily in earnest in their devotion to the Word of God and the Kingdom of Christ, that your good health and ability may be very useful and comforting to us all, especially in the midst of the strange perils that are now overhanging us. But if God indeed wishes that you should thus be sick, his will will most certainly be better than all our wills, just as it was needful that even the very best and innocent

---

* Briefe. De Wette., 4, 563 ff.

will of his dear Son should be subject to the higher and supremely good will of the dear Father. His will be done also in us with joy, or at least with patience. Amen. In the Word of God we read: 'Be of good cheer, I have overcome the world!' How can we do otherwise, than glorify and bear in our body the Conqueror of the world, the devil, sin, death, the flesh, diseases and all evils. His yoke, we know, is easy, and his burden is sweet. But our yoke and burden, which he bore for us, was the devil, yea, and the wrath of God. From that may God preserve us! Yea, he has already delivered us from it, and we bear instead his dear load and his sweet burden. Ah! *that* we have yet to undertake, and joyfully to accept the change. It is a kind merchant and a gracious dealer, who sells us life for death, righteousness for sin, and demands for interest only a sickness or two, enduring for a moment, as evidence that he gives more cheaply and lends more kindly than brokers and dealers on the earth. Yea, truly! the Lord Jesus Christ is the Man, and the true Man, who struggles and conquers and triumphs in us. He must and shall still live, and we with him and in him. There can be no other issue of the strife, however the gates of hell may rage. Therefore, as you desire a message of comfort from me, I offer this as my comfort in Christ: that you may be joyously thankful to the Father of all grace, who has called you to his light and to the confession of his Son, and given to you abundantly at least this grace, that you do not favor the enemies of his Son, nor advance their plans, which you could not indeed do unless Cochleus, Vicelius, and Albert of Halle pleased you better than St. Paul or Isaac, or just as well, which I trust they do not. What does it matter, then, that God lays you upon your bed and sends sickness upon you, since he grants you such abundant grace and has separated and chosen you out of such diabolic darkness and such a hellish rabble? Thank him, and render the interest due like an honest man, and pay your vows, as the 116th Psalm says (v. 10): 'I believe, and therefore am I thus afflicted: but how can I repay what God has done for me? I will drink the cup of joy, and praise and thank the name of my Lord,' *i. e.*, I will bear misfortune and sufferings with joyfulness and sing out above them hallelujah. Do this and you shall live. Christ, our Lord, who has begun in you his work, will carry it on to a blessed end, as with us all, although we are poor sinners. He himself knows our weakness, and his Spirit intercedes for us. To him do I now earnestly commend you.

Just see now, have I not afflicted my patient far enough? My Lord, Katie, sends greeting, and hopes that you may soon be well and come to see us.

"MARTINUS LUTHER, D."

Wittenberg, Tuesday Vigiliæ Catharinæ (Nov. 24th), in the year 1534.

To Frederick Myconius, Superintendent at Gotha, who lay dying of consumption, he addressed the following heroic epistle: "Grace and Peace. I have, dear Frederick, received your letter, in which you inform me that you are lying sick unto death, or, as you rightly and in a true Christian spirit explain, 'sick unto life.' Now, although it gives me a peculiar joy, that you are so unterrified in view of death, which is for all the pious but an ordinary sleep; yea, so full of desire to depart and be with Christ, as we should all be, not only when on beds of languishing, but even in the fullest vigor of life, at every time, at every place, under all circumstances, as becomes us Christians, who have already been with Christ awakened, made alive, and admitted to heavenly enjoyments, who are even judges of the angels, so that nothing remains to be done, but that the veil and the dark word be removed—although, I say, it has afforded me a peculiar joy to learn this of you, yet I beseech and implore the Lord Jesus, our Life, our Salvation and our Health, that he may not permit yet this evil to fall upon me, that I should survive and see you and others of our friends break through the veil and enter into rest, leaving me behind, out among the devils, to be vexed yet longer after your escape. I have surely been vexed enough through so many years, and might be accounted worthy and deserving to go before you. I pray, therefore, that the Lord may let me become sick in your stead, and give me commandment to lay aside this my robe of flesh, that is no longer good for anything, that has served its time and is worn out. I recognize plainly enough that I am no longer good for anything. Hence I beseech you also to pray with us to the Lord, that he may preserve you longer for service in his church and to the mockery of the devil. For you surely see, and he who is our Life also sees, what talents and persons are necessary for his church. Farewell, my Frederick, and may the Lord grant that I may never while I live hear of your departure, but may he ordain that you survive me. This I pray, this I desire, and may my will be done, Amen; for this my will seeks the honor of God's name, and not my own pleasure or honor. Again, farewell. We are praying most earnestly for you. My Katie sends greeting, as do all the others, who are deeply affected by your sickness.

"Your MARTIN LUTHER."*

Sunday after Epiphany, 1541.

We can understand why the Elector, John Frederick, when, in June, 1540, Melanchthon lay dying at Weimar, would hear of no other course than to bring Luther, traveling day and night, from Wittenberg. "When the latter arrived," reports Ratzeberger,† "he found Melanchthon really in such condition as had been reported to him. His eyes had already become dim, reason had entirely vanished, the power of speech was lost, hearing was gone, and his countenance and temples were sunken. It was, indeed, as Luther said, the Hypocratic face. He recognized no one, ate and drank nothing. When Luther first looked upon him, he was shocked beyond measure, and said to his companions: 'God forbid! how has the devil marred this instrument!' and, turning immediately to the window, he prayed earnestly to God. 'Then and there,' Luther afterwards said, 'was our Lord God

---

* Myconius, always sickly from the year 1541, did in fact not die until after Luther's death, i. e., on April 7th, 1546, and was accustomed to acknowledge that this letter of Luther had given him a new lease of life.

† Luther und seine Zeit. Published by Neudecker, p. 103 f.

obliged to listen to me, for I cast my burden before his door, and besieged his ear with all the promises to answer prayer that I could repeat from the Holy Scriptures, so that he was obliged to hear me, if I was at all to trust his promises.' He then took Philip by the hand, and said: 'Be of good courage, Philip, you will not die. Although God has reason enough to take away your life, yet he does not desire the death of the sinner, but that he may turn from his ways and live. He has pleasure in life and not in death. If God called and received again to his favor the very greatest sinners that ever lived on earth, Adam and Eve, much less will he cast you out, my Philip, or suffer you to perish in sin and sorrow. Therefore do not give way to despondency, and thus become your own murderer, but trust in the Lord, who is able to kill and make alive again.' For Luther well understood the troubles of his friend's heart and conscience. As he was thus holding and addressing him, Philip began to breathe again, but was still for a long time not able to talk. He then turned his face directly toward Luther, and began to entreat him for God's sake not to detain him any longer, saying that he was upon a good journey and that he should allow him to go on, as nothing better could happen to him. 'By no means, Philip,' said Luther, 'you must serve our Lord God yet further here.' Thus Philip became more and more animated, and Luther, ordering some food to be quickly prepared, took it to him himself. But Philip refused to eat of it. Luther, however, compelled him with threats, and said: 'Do you hear, Philip? Quick! You must eat now, or I will excommunicate you!' By this language he was prevailed upon to eat a little, and thus gradually regained strength."

The Electress Elizabeth, of Brandenburg, who had fled for protection to her uncle, John the Steadfast, because her husband, as was commonly reported, intended to imprison her for secretly receiving the holy communion in both elements at Easter, 1528,* and to whom the castle at Lichtenburg had been assigned as a residence, acted not unwisely when, in 1537, she secured admission to Luther's house, in order that both her temporal and her spiritual wants might there be ministered to during her great bodily weakness.† His Katie sat upon the bed by her side and soothed her, and he himself gave her every possible attention.‡ She was there restored again to health.‖

* Briefe. De Wette, 3, 296.
† Ibid., 6. 445.
‡ Ibid., 6, 188.
‖ Ibid., 5, 596 f.

CHAPTER III.

HOW LUTHER INTERESTED HIMSELF IN THE FORLORN.

THE first among the many destitute and forlorn in whose behalf Luther was called upon to interest himself were those who, for the sake of the Gospel which he had restored to them, had, with cheerful trust in God, forsaken the monasteries in which they had been incarcerated, or the positions which they had held in the Roman Catholic church. To Wittenberg they came, not only from the various provinces of Germany, but also from the Netherlands,* France† and other lands. They looked to the Man whose word had awakened their consciences and illuminated their hearts, not only for further instruction, but also, since they had forsaken all for the faith, for food and shelter, in fact for their entire support. The Reformer recognized his duty, and, despite his many other engagements, applied himself with the greatest diligence to its discharge. His first con-

---

* Briefe. De Wette, 2, 182.
† Ibid., 2, 302 ; 3, 102 (Two superiors at once).

cern was to secure for the refugees admission into respectable and suitable homes. He then notified their nearest relatives, and inquired what these were willing to do.* As was to be expected, the majority refused to assume any responsibility for their escaped friends. Not only were the monasteries very commonly regarded as institutions for the support of poor relations, but very many yet clung so tenaciously to the old church, that they condemned the forsaking of these spiritual houses as a horrible and heaven-offending crime. It now became necessary so to locate those who were forsaken by their friends, that they might earn their own living.

The priests who had been compelled to flee on account of their faith could be easily provided for, for the most of the old pastors in the territory of the Elector of Saxony were entirely incapable, if not altogether unworthy men. Luther was constantly sending to his friend, the very influential Spalatin, for the good of the Church, such confessors of the faith, tried in the fires of affliction. If he knew of no appropriate position for his man in the territory of his own ruler, having intimate relations with many princes and cities throughout Germany, he sought at a distance what he could

* Briefe. De Wette, 2, 319; 3 33.

not find near at hand. He thus sent to Count Philip of Nassau-Weilburg, in 1538, Johann Beyer of Steinach, an able preacher, who had withdrawn from the ungodly monastery at Halle, together with his wife and child.*

It was much more difficult to make secure provision for the future of the escaped monks. Scarcely any of these had received sufficient spiritual training and culture to make them available as preachers of the Gospel. But whenever Luther discovered a competent man, he spoke a good word for him. He thus, for example, secured from Spalatin for the brother Moritz, who had left the monastery at Altenburg, the pastorate of Schönewalde, near Herzberg,† and very earnestly recommended the brother of his own order, Gabriel Zwilling, to the council of Altenburg as a suitable man to be called as their minister.‡ In most cases, it was necessary to advise the learning of an honorable trade, and to point out the proper steps and furnish the means to this end. Luther here displayed keen penetration and great practical ability. He thus recommended to his friend, Hans of Dolzig, as a good gardener, Ern Heinrich, who, unlike the

---

* Briefe. De Wette, 3, 344; 6, 204.
† Ibid., 2, 361.
‡ Ibid., 2, 183.

others who left the monastery, had received a hundred guldens.* "As Wittenberg," however, "swarmed with escaped monks, and others were daily arriving," as Luther himself writes,† it was necessary for him to call his distant friends to his aid. Nicholas Hausmann, at that time pastor at Zwickau, where cloth-making and linen-weaving were extensively carried on,‡ rendered him faithful assistance. A short letter of the Reformer, in which he recommends to him such a former monk, has been preserved.§ Since, however, the factories would receive no one as an apprentice without evidence of legitimate birth, and as the appropriate testimonials were very commonly refused to former inmates of the monasteries in order to compel them to re-enter the hated walls, Luther frequently found himself called upon to testify that the applicant, according to his best knowledge and conscientious belief, was "born and descended from reputable and irreproachable parents" and had conducted himself reputably and honorably, and that no one could accuse him of anything to the contrary. With such a testimonial, for example, he dismisses Gregory Morgenstern of Dresden, a former Augustinian, who,

---

* Briefe. De Wette, 3, 164.   † Ibid., 2, 241.
‡ Ibid., 2, 251.   § Ibid., 2, 241.

"according to Christian doctrine and the counsel of truth, desires to be transferred forthwith from his perilous condition to a blessed condition, since he wishes, in all honor before God, by the help of pious people, to support himself, like all the sons of Adam, by the sweat of his face."*

But it was the most difficult task of all, to give proper counsel and care to the escaped nuns. Luther could not, of course, as long as he was unmarried, receive any destitute nun into the monastery. He often did so afterwards, and one of these, "Aunt Lene," an aunt of his wife, whose full name was Magdelene von Bora, for whom he had warm rooms specially prepared, remained with him until her happy death.† The Duchess Ursula of Münsterberg, who had almost miraculously escaped from the convent at Freiberg, found with him a refuge of righteousness. "She is now staying at my house," writes he to Spalatin on the 20th of October, 1528,‡ "with two young women, one of whom, Margaretha Volkmar, is the daughter of a citizen of Leipzig, and the other, Dorothea, the daughter of a Freiberg citizen, who took with her into the convent 1400 guldens inherited

---

* Briefe. De Wette, 2, 413.
† Ibid., 6, 327.
‡ Ibid., 3, 390 f.

from her father, and has left this behind her, in poverty to follow the poor Christ with Madam Ursula. The whole party have brought not a single penny with them." For very many of these escaped nuns suitable places were found, as for Aunt Lene, in various homes, as assistants in housekeeping and the care of children. Others were so fortunate as to secure good husbands, and preside over their own households. Even here Luther very often smoothed the way, as, for example, he had at first designed his own future wife for Jerome Baumgärtner, the son of a Nuremberg patrician,* and, when this failed, for Caspar Glatz, vicar of the pastorate of Orlamund.†

Many young women of the convents asked his counsel as to whether and under what circumstances it was allowable to forsake a convent, as, for example, those to whom he replied on the 6th of August, 1524.‡ Many an escaped nun, likewise, sought his counsel in regard to her contemplated marriage. He was always accommodating, but cautious as well. "Grace and Peace. Decorous and dear Maiden, Hannah," he writes under such circumstances on the 14th day of December, 1523,§

---

* Briefe. De Wette, 2, 553.
† Beste, Kath. von Bora, p. 23.
‡ Briefe. De Wette, 2, 534 ff.
§ Ibid., 2, 445.

"I have received your letter, and, as you desire, will do my best, both with Mr. S. von K., and with any others who may ask my opinion, to help on your proposed or promised marriage, that it may move along right smoothly. God knows that, so far as in me lies, I would most willingly help every one along in much smaller matters than this, if I were able. I am not at all displeased to hear that you are thinking of marriage. But in such matters I cannot at such a distance pass judgment either one way or the other. More than one person is here concerned, and we are forbidden by God to pass judgment upon petition of but one of the parties in any matter. In this I, just like yourself, make no distinction on account of rank. One human being is worthy of another, if they only delight in and love one another, so that the enemy may not deceive them. You need therefore have no doubt, but that I shall be present, when it comes to the time, or, if asked about the matter, will speak most favorably, and in every way help to make it move along smoothly. For, since I observe that you are well pleased with it, it shall, so far as I am concerned, provided no one else is injured by it, be undisturbed and unhindered. But do not forget to seek God's blessing also, that not merely natural affection, but also the favor of his grace, may be yours. May he be gracious to you and to your dear lover. Amen."

Now and then Luther was enabled to make use of a former nun, although not as a deaconess in the church (it is remarkable, that it occurred to no one to thus appropriate the very prevalent term, "the maid-servants of Christ," although for very many no employment whatever could .be found!), yet for service in schools for girls, in the establishment of which he was greatly interested.

"Grace and Peace in Christ Jesus," thus he addresses,* on Thursday after Agapetus (August, 18), 1527, the young woman, Else of Kanitz, one of the eight nuns who had escaped with Catharine von Bora from the convent of Nimbsch, near Grimma,† "Decorous, virtuous Maiden, Else. I have by letter requested your dear Aunt Hannah, of Plausig, ‡ to send you to me for a while; for I have had it in mind to make use of you, in setting you to teach young girls, and to begin with you such work as an example for others. You are to make your home with me, and eat at my table, so

---

* Briefe. De Wette, 3, 170.

† Ibid., 2, 319.

‡ Seidemann's supposition is probably correct, that this Hannah of Plausig is one and the same person with the above-mentioned nun, Hannah. Briefe. De Wette, 6, 688.

that you will be in no danger and have no care; I beg of you therefore not to refuse me this favor. I hear also that the wicked enemy is assailing you with grievous thoughts. O, my dear Maiden, do not be terrified by that, for whoever endures the devil here will not have to suffer in the other world. It is a good sign. Christ also suffered all such things, as did many holy prophets and apostles, as you know the Psalter teaches us. Therefore be of good cheer, and endure willingly such chastisement from the Father, who will also in his own time help you to escape from it. When you come, I will say more to you about this. Herewith I commend you to God. Amen."

Among the Forlorn we mention also those who on account of their profession of faith in the Gospel were forsaken of men, endured grievous persecutions, or were even cast into prison. With the utmost fidelity did Luther exert himself in behalf of such. Two examples will furnish sufficient evidence of this. The above-mentioned Felicitas of Selmenitz, who was comforted in her sickness by the noble man of God at Wittenberg, had already passed through many trying experiences. Her husband, Wolf, of Selmenitz, formerly owner of the Vitzenburg Castle on the Unstrut and warden at Allstedt, had been foully assassinated before the inn of Moritz Knebel, known as "The Golden Ring," at Halle, on the 9th of January, 1519.* She had remained living there and had found her comfort in the Word of God. She became heartily attached to the Gospel doctrine, and boldly took the holy communion in both elements. In 1527 she moved with her son to Wittenberg, but the pestilence drove her back within a few weeks to Halle. She was then required by the Elector of Mentz, Cardinal Albrecht, who, as the Archbishop of Magdeburg, had control also of Halle, either to surrender her faith or to leave Halle. The forlorn woman applied to Luther, the faithful counselor and provider of all the forlorn. She very soon received from him the desired advice.†

"Grace and Peace in Christ, our Lord and Saviour. Discreet, virtuous Madam. I have received and considered your appeal. Christ will be with you and will not forsake you. As to your question, whether you should flee or remain, it is my opinion that you are at perfect liberty to flee and can do so with a good conscience, since you have received permission from those in authority; but still I would rather see you remain for a while yet, until you receive more positive information as

---

* Kreysig, Beiträge zur Historie der Sächs. Lande, 2, 101.
† Briefe. De Wette, 3, 297.

to whether the Cardinal will really come, in order that no one may regard your flight as premature or without occasion. Yet I leave it all to your judgment. May God, according to his divine will, strengthen you and all the brethren and sisters at Halle. MARTINUS LUTHER.

"*Wittenberg, April 1st, 1528.*"

With this faithful witness for Christ he remained in constant communication,* and selected her, as it appears, at a later period as sponsor for one of his children. In 1534 he wrote in her Bible, still preserved in the St. Mary's library in Halle:

"Jn. v. Search the Scriptures, for they testify of me.

"Ps. ii. Blessed are all who put their trust in him.

"Isa. vii. If ye believe not, ye shall not abide. That is, everything will be a failure for you which you undertake without faith, even though in itself it were pure wisdom, power, art or wealth; for God will not suffer it to prosper.

"To the beloved Sponsor of my child, the discreet, virtuous Lady, Felicitas of Selmenitz.

"MARTINUS LUTHER, D."

* She took a meal with him on the 10th of September, 1538. See Colloquia, Ed. Bindseil, 2, 165.

Evidently the passages here quoted were designed to be for this lady what guiding-stars are to the forlorn wanderers in the desert.

Leonard Kaiser, a priest, who had succeeded in escaping from prison and had come to Wittenberg, was arrested by the Abbot of Passau, while upon a visit to his dying father, and placed in bonds. Luther took an interest in the lonely prisoner, and on the 20th of May, 1527, sent him the following letter:*

"Grace, Strength and Peace in Christ. Your old man is imprisoned, my Leonard, according to God's will and the calling of Christ our Lord, who also gave his new man for you and your sins into the hands of the ungodly, that he by his blood might release you and make you his brother and a joint heir with him of everlasting life. We are very sorry for you, and pray diligently that you may be set free, in order that you may live, not for yourself but for others, to the honor of God, if it be his will. But should it not be the will of your Father in Heaven that you be set free, yet see to it that you, with a spirit at perfect liberty, bravely and steadfastly conquer this affliction of Satan, or at least endure it, through the power of Christ. He is with you in your imprisonment and will be

---

* Briefe. De Wette, 3, 179 f.

with you also in every trial, as he has himself faithfully and kindly promised, saying: 'I am with him in trouble' (Ps. xci. 15). It is necessary, therefore, that you with confidence call upon him in prayer, and that you encourage and confirm yourself with psalms of consolation in the midst of this snorting of Satan; so that you may become strong in the Lord, and not speak any too humbly or timidly in the teeth of Behemoth, as though you were overcome and feared the proud might of Satan. But you must call upon Christ, who is everywhere present and mighty; and must defy and mock the rage and arrogance of Satan, well assured that he shall not be able to injure you, and all the less the more he rages, as Paul says: 'If God be for us, who can be against us?' (Rom. viii. 31). 'All things are put under his feet' (Ps. viii. 6). He can help all who are tempted, who has himself also been tempted in all points. Therefore, my dearest Brother, grow strong in the Lord, and be strong in the power of his might, in order that, whether you be now set free or not, you may yet with a willing heart recognize, bear, carry out and praise the paternal will of God concerning you. That you may endeavor to do this to the praise of his Gospel, may the Father of our Lord Jesus Christ, the Father of mercy and the

God of all comfort, grant according to the riches of his glorious grace. Amen. In him, farewell. Pray for us."

But not only single persons found themselves in forlorn condition. Whole companies of believers, entire congregations, turned in vain for help and protection to those who should in justice have interested themselves in their behalf. Luther, though at a distance, exerted himself as a true shepherd in behalf of these, who had been forsaken, if not actually persecuted, by their own appointed shepherds, leading them to the living water, and preparing a table before them in the presence of their enemies. What remarkable facility he displayed in doing this, is manifest from his letters. Here again, two must suffice.

To the Elect, the Beloved of God, all the Members of Christ at Augsburg, his dear Masters and Brethren, he indited on the 11th of December, 1523, this epistle:*

"Grace and Peace in Christ our Lord. It has come to our ears, dear Brethren and Masters, that some among you have innocently fallen into difficulty on account of the marriage of a priest,† and,

---

* Briefe. De Wette, 2, 440, ff.

† The priest, Jacob Griessbüttel, for whose marriage the authorities had refused to open the church, had, in the pres-

besides the injury, are made to endure also ridicule and reproach from those who rejoice when Christ is crucified, and laugh when their father's distress and nakedness are uncovered. But, now that we are by the grace of God in the communion of the saints and members one of another, we must, as Paul says (Rom. xii. 13, 15), minister to the necessity of the saints, and have sympathy for those who suffer. For, just as St. Paul says again (1 Cor. xii. 26): 'Whether one member suffereth, all the others suffer with it; or one member is honored, all the others rejoice;' so, whether there be among you honor or dishonor, peace or tribulation, we account these as our own and are equally affected by them. We depend also likewise upon you, Beloved, that our joy may be your joy, and our misfortune yours, on account of the common faith and Word, with which God has in his great mercy endowed us. Therefore I could not and ought not to neglect to exhort you and to comfort you with the comfort wherewith we are comforted of God through his holy Word, in order that you may not only bear the present trial with patience, but also become vigorous and strong to await and

ence of 32 adherents of the evangelical doctrines, at a feast, made the declaration, that he then and there took the bride to be his wife. Comp. Uhlhorn, Urban Rhegius, p. 57.

to overcome yet greater things, although I do not imagine that you stand in need of my poor epistle.

"In the first place, Paul says (Rom. viii. 17; 2 Tim. ii. 12): 'If we would reign with him, we must also suffer with him.' For, if we take pleasure in the Gospel and desire to become partakers of his unspeakable riches and his eternal treasure, we must also take into account his cross, and the tribulation that comes with it, considering that his riches and treasure are eternal and his tribulation temporal, yea, but momentary. He has himself declared (Jn. xvi. 33): 'In the world ye shall have tribulation, but in me ye shall have peace.' If we would have peace in him, then we must have tribulation from the world. The words of Christ can have no other meaning. Remember my word, says he, which I have spoken to you: 'The servant is not better than his lord. If they have persecuted me, they will persecute you also.' A slothful and unprofitable servant indeed would he be, who should wish to sit upon a silk cushion and live in luxury, while his master was without, hungering and toiling and contending against his enemies. That would be a foolish merchant indeed, who should throw away his gold and silver and have nothing to do with it, because it was tied up, not in silk and satin, but in rough, dirty bags and sacks; or who should become disgusted with his treasure because it was heavy, and not as light as a feather. It is the very nature of treasures to be heavy, and to increase in weight according to their value; and it is not customary to carry gold and silver in beautiful bags and sacks, but in black, rough, dirty cloth, which no one would otherwise like to have about his body.

"Just so is it also with our treasure. It is indeed great, precious, costly and noble, but we must carry it in tribulation and sufferings; these are its weight and the dirty bags in which it lies hidden. If now any one should attempt to carry this treasure about publicly in beautiful bags, i. e., wants to be a Christian, and yet to be splendidly supported, to have pleasure and honor and good friends, and not be despised, nor have to endure in consequence sorrow, shame, injury and enemies; what else can he expect but that he will be robbed of his treasure? Why, he is carrying it grandly and publicly and visibly, whereas it is the nature of this treasure to be well concealed under shame, injury and sufferings, as in a sooty bag or sack, in order that the world may not recognize or steal it, which comes to pass when the world begins to honor, love and assist us on account of our treasure. Therefore Christ says (Matt. xiii. 44) that the man who found the treasure in the field hid and buried it again. The meaning of this is, that it is not possible nor to be desired, that the Gospel should shine forth and soar aloft in great honors, comfort, pleasure and wealth, for thus it would be lost; but it must be hidden and buried under tribulation and shame, in order that it may not shine forth before the world and seek to please it, for thus it remains safe and free.

"God is therefore very graciously regarding you, and protecting your treasure, in order to preserve it to you, for which you should suitably thank and praise him with rejoicing, that he accounts you worthy to hold such treasure, and now also to put it into the right bag, that it may not be lost. Therefore be of good cheer, my dear Masters and Brethren; it is well with you, and better times will come. Only fall not away, out of the hand of God, who has now laid hold of you to make good, honest Christians out of you, that you may not in word alone, as I, alas! and others in your circumstances, but in deed and in truth, live according to the Gospel.

"It is written (Isa. lxiv. 8): 'We are his clay; he is our potter.' The clay must not control the art and the hand of the potter, but must let itself be controlled and shaped. Therefore the Gospel applies its square, which St. Paul has given it: the word of the cross (1 Cor. i. 8). He who will not have the cross, must do without the word. It is true, there could be nothing more delightful in Heaven or on earth than the word without the cross. But the pleasure would not last long, since nature cannot long endure unmixed joy and pleasure, as it is said: 'Man can bear everything except prosperity,' and: 'It takes strong legs to carry prosperity.'

"Therefore God has seasoned this sweet, delightful treasure for us a little, and poured in vinegar and myrrh to give it a sharp taste, that we might not become satiated with it. 'Bitter makes the meal,' they say; and thus also tribulation on earth makes our hearts so much the more cheerful, keen and eager to enjoy this treasure; for thereby we taste and discover its power to comfort the heart in God. Hence, also, Solomon calls it mixed wine, Prov. ix. 5, where wisdom says: 'Come and drink the wine which I have mixed for you;' and in Ps. lxxv. 9 we read: 'The Lord has in his hand a cup full of mixed wine.' It is a pure wine, which intoxicates the soul, but yet so mixed with sufferings as to remain pleasant to the taste.

"But why should I say more? You yourselves know very well, Beloved, that the Word of God is everywhere in the Scriptures represented as bringing with it in this world tribulation, shame and all manner of trials, but as setting forth at the same time also, for admonition and comfort, how very precious this treasure of our faith is, and how greatly its value is increased by such trials. You are therefore yourselves abundantly able to comfort one another, and what I have ventured to do must be considered as a piece of presumption. Yet, because I see that God has granted to you the same riches as to us through the knowledge of our Lord Jesus Christ, I cannot refrain from acting foolishly, and, out of the joy and pleasure that I find in your fellowship, thus talking to you and exhorting you, although I myself stand greatly in need of both admonition and instruction. I beg you, therefore, Beloved, to excuse this impertinent, but well-meant letter, and commend me, weak, poor, frail vessel to God in your prayers. Permit me also, I pray, to commend to you all our messengers. May the God of all grace, who has begun to reveal himself to you and to renew the likeness of his Son in you, abundantly complete his work, according to the riches of his glory, both in you and in us, until the day of our Lord Jesus Christ, for whose coming to deliver us from all the remains of evil in this flesh we confidently wait. Amen. The grace of God be with you all. Amen."

In February of the following year, Luther had occasion to address a letter of consolation to the adherents of the Gospel at Miltenberg on the Main. Johann Draconites, so named from the place of his birth, according to the custom of the time, also known as Johann Carlstadt, had there introduced the Gospel with great success, and thus stirred up the wrath of the civil ruler, the Elector Albrecht of Mentz. The pastor was driven out, and his chief adherents arrested and put to death. Luther manifested the warmest and deepest interest. To all the dear friends of Christ at Miltenberg he wrote:*

"Grace and Peace from God the Father and from the Lord Jesus Christ. The holy apostle Paul, when he wished to comfort his brethren at Corinth, began thus (2 Cor. i. 3, 4): 'Blessed be God, the Father of our Lord Jesus Christ, the Father of mercy and God of all comfort, who comforteth us in all our affliction, that we may be able also to comfort those who are in affliction with the comfort wherewith we are comforted of God.' In these words the apostle teaches by his own example that we are to comfort the afflicted; yet in such a

* Briefe. De Wette, 2, 475 ff.

way that the comfort may come not from men but from God. This he adds, it is very evident, in order to guard against that false, shameful comfort which the world, the flesh and even the devil give, and by which all the benefit and fruit of the cross are destroyed and hindered. But what that comfort is which comes from God, he points out (Rom. xv. 4): 'Whatsoever has been written, has been written for our instruction, that we through patience and comfort of the Scriptures might have hope.' He says: 'might have hope;' but to have hope is to be concerned for that which we do not see nor feel (Rom. viii. 24). Worldly comfort aims to see and feel that which the afflicted one desires, and will have nothing to do with patience; but here must patience remain with comfort of the Scriptures in hope.

"Just in this way does St. Paul really treat his brethren at Corinth. When he has spoken to them of the comfort of God, he begins at length to praise them as an epistle of Christ, wrought by his preaching of the Gospel and written by the living Spirit (2 Cor. iii. 4), and breaks out in a lofty hymn in praise of the Gospel, so that a carnally-minded person hearing him might well think: Is this man drunken, that, when he wishes to comfort the Corinthians, he should thus only glorify himself and his preaching and extol his Gospel? But whoever rightly considers it, can understand that the beloved Paul is drawing the true, noble comfort from the Scriptures, and making them strong and joyous through the Gospel.

"I have accordingly also, my dear Friends, undertaken to comfort your hearts in your affliction with such comfort as I have received from God, for I have been very fully informed by your exiled pastor, Dr. Johann Carlstadt, and through other sources, how the enemies of the Gospel and assassins of souls have dealt with you on account of the Word of God, which they in their infamous blasphemy now call Lutheran doctrine, in order to make it appear that they are doing God service, in seeking to destroy the doctrines of men, just as the Jews, fulfilling the prophecy of Christ, treated the apostles.

"It would be a worldly comfort, which could be of no benefit whatever, but altogether injurious to your souls and to the cause, if you and I should seek comfort in avenging ourselves upon the blasphemers by scolding and mourning over their impiety and wickedness. And though we should even slay them all with our hands, or banish them, or had the pleasure and delight of seeing them punished by some one else on account of the suffering inflicted upon us, there would yet be nothing thereby accomplished. For this is worldly revenge and comfort, and does not befit us; but it is befitting to our enemies, as you now see that they, having cooled their malice upon you and avenged themselves, are merry over it, and are wonderfully comforted. But what sort of comfort is that? Have they any hope? Have they any patience? Have they any Scripture? Verily, instead of God, they have used their fists; instead of patience, they have shown revenge; instead of hope, they have given vent to their malice openly and have already received all the good things that they will ever have. Whence comes then such comfort? It does not come from God, and must therefore certainly come from the devil. And so it does. But what will be the end of the comfort that comes from the devil? Paul says (Phil. iii. 19): 'Their boasting shall come to a shameful end.'

"See now what a rich, proud comfort arises out of this for you! In the first place, you are certain that it is for the sake of God's Word that you endure their insolence and abuse. What matters it that they call it heresy? You are sure that it is God's Word; they cannot therefore be sure that it is heresy. They will not hear nor receive it; they cannot therefore prove it to be heresy. Yet they go on slandering and persecuting, upon such uncertain ground, as St. Peter says (2 Pet. ii. 12), 'What they do not understand!' Hence they cannot have a good conscience in the matter; but you have a secure, certain conviction that you are suffering for God's sake. Now who can ever fully describe what a blessed, proud comfort it is, to be certain that one is suffering for God's sake? For who suffers? Whom does it concern? Who will avenge it, if we suffer for God's sake? Well does St. Peter say (1 Pet. iii. 14): 'Blessed are ye, if ye suffer for righteousness' sake.' If one were the emperor of the whole world, he should not only be willing cheerfully to surrender his throne to secure such sufferings, but should even count it as dung, compared with such comforting treasure.

"You have really, therefore, dear Friends, no occasion to desire revenge, nor to wish evil to your enemies, but much rather to regard them with heartfelt compassion. For you have in fact been already too highly avenged, to say nothing of that which yet awaits them at the end. They have already suffered altogether too much. To you they have done only a kindness, that you should be led by their raging to the comfort of God; to themselves they have done an injury, from which they can scarcely, and some of them never, recover.

"For what does it matter, that they have tormented you for a little while in your body and your earthly possessions? That will soon be over. And what does it matter, that they for a little while rejoice in their wantonness? It cannot last long. Consider, in the meantime, your happiness and their misery. You have a good, secure conscience and a just cause; they have an evil, uncertain conscience and a blind cause, of which they do not even yet know how unjust it is. You have therefore the comfort of God with patience out of the Scriptures in hope; they have therefore the comfort of the devil through revenge in visible wantonness.

"If now the privilege were given you to choose between their portion and your own, would you not run and flee from their side, as from the devil, even though it were a very heaven, and hasten to your portion, even though it were a very hell? For heaven could not be joyous, if the devil reigned there, and hell could not be gloomy, if God reigned there.

"Therefore, dear Friends, would you avenge and comfort yourselves right well and proudly, not only upon your visible, bodily persecutors, but upon the devil, who rides them, then treat him thus: Be right joyful, and thank God that you have been made worthy to hear and understand his Word, and to suffer for it, and be content to know certainly that your cause is God's Word and your comfort from God. Pity your enemies, who have no good conscience in their cause, but only the miserable, gloomy comfort of the devil through their insolence, impatience, revenge and earthly malice. Believe assuredly that you will by such a joyful spirit, praise and thanksgiving, grieve their god, the devil, more than if you were to slay a thousand of your enemies. For it is not his aim to comfort them and give you bodily pain, but he wants to make you sad and melancholy, so that you may be of no service to God. Keep on, therefore, all the more, and mock him, that his scheme may fail and be given up in disgust.

"Yet one thing more let me point out to you, that will wonderfully nettle him, and that he fears most of all. He knows very well that. there is a little verse in the Psalter (viii. 2), which reads: 'Thou hast laid a strong foundation through the mouth of babes and sucklings, that thou mightest make an end of the enemy and the avenger!' This verse threatens him not alone with grief and misery, but with total destruction, and that, not by means of some great power, which would still be an honor for him, but by means of helpless sucklings, in whom there is no strength. It stings the mighty, proud enemy, and gives him dreadful pain, that his great power, his terrible raging, his wrathful vengeance, is to be cast down into the dust by childish weakness, without power, and that he cannot prevent it.

In this let us help, and do our part with zeal. We are babes and sucklings, if we are weak and let the enemies exercise their might and power over us, saying and doing upon their part whatever they please, whilst we upon our part keep silence, as though we were unable to do or say anything—we as little children, and they as powerful heroes and giants. But yet, meanwhile, God speaks through our mouth his Word, which glorifies his power. This is such a rock and firm foundation, that the gates of hell can avail nothing against it. Wherever this remains and has free course, some of the enemies, who were the devil's scales, are at length converted. When these scales are now stripped off of him by the Word of God, he is left naked and weak; and thus it comes to pass, as this verse says, that an end is made of the enemy and the avenger. This is a joyful victory and a conquest without sword or fist. It therefore gives the devil great pain. It is very pleasant and agreeable to him, when he is able through his servants to stir us up to wrath, revenge, impatience and sadness; but where the only results are joy and the praising of God and glorifying of his Word, that is a real hell for him.

"Yes, some one may say, but it is forbidden, upon penalty of life and property, to speak the Word of God. Well, let him that is strong refuse to keep such commandment; for they have no authority to forbid any one. God's Word ought to be, it shall and must be, unbound. But if any one is too timid and weak, I will give him another counsel, namely, that he shall yet rejoice in secret, thank God and glorify his Word, as we have said before, and pray to God for strength to speak it also openly, that the enemy and the avenger may be put to confusion. To this end, I present to you this 120th Psalm, translated into German and briefly explained, that you may see what comfort God offers you through his Word, and how you ought to pray against the false revilers and raging persecutors.

'*Psalm* cxx.

'1. I cried unto the Lord in my distress, and he heareth me.

'2. Lord, deliver my soul from wicked mouths and from false tongues.

'3. What shall one give unto thee, and what shall one do against false tongues?

'4. Sharp arrows of the mighty, with coals of juniper.

'5. Ah, my sorrow! that I must so long wander! I dwell among the tents of Kedar.

'6. My soul must dwell so long among them that hate peace.

'7. I kept the peace, but when I spoke, they took up stones.'

"The first verse teaches us to whom we should go when misfortune overtakes us: not to the emperor, not to the sword, not to our own counsel or wisdom, but to the Lord, who is the true and only helper in the time of need. 'I cried,' says he, 'unto the Lord in my distress.' And that we should do this boldly and joyously, and doing so, shall not fail, he indicates when he says: 'And he heareth me,' as though he should say: The Lord desires that we should go to him in our distress, and he is willing to hear and to help.

"The second verse presents the grievance and indicates what the distress is: not that God did not know it beforehand, but that we may be thus stirred up and driven to pray the more diligently. It is just the very same distress which has fallen upon you at Miltenberg, and others like you in German countries, namely, that wicked mouths and false tongues will not endure the Word of

God, but hold on to their human vanity and lies, and command us to keep silence, that their wicked, false, poisonous doctrine may alone be preached.

"The third verse holds a consultation as to how and by what means the matter may be helped. For human timidity desires and longs for help and protection in the world, and many are greatly concerned about these, as this verse with its looking about for counsel indicates. But the Spirit casts this all aside, and will have nothing to do with such helps, as is plain from what follows.

"The fourth verse mentions the true help, namely, 'Sharp arrows of the mighty,' *i. e.*, that God should send powerful preachers who should speak his Word boldly. These are the arrows of God, and they are sharp, when they pierce, and do not spare, but shoot and wound all human vanities. By this means, false tongues are overcome and changed into true, Christian tongues. 'Coals of juniper,' are true Christians, who show forth in their lives the Word of God which is declared by the sharp arrows, and make it burn in ardent, fervent love manifested by works. For it is said that coals of juniper do really keep a fire well. This verse therefore wishes for skillful preachers, who shall employ the Word of God powerfully in faith, and smite to the earth every device of the devil, and let their faith burn and shine in works of fervent love. For there are indeed in these times many preachers of the Word, but they are not mighty and do not preach powerfully. And although they preach the Word, they do not make it sharp; for they spare where there should be no sparing, *i. e.*, the great multitude. Furthermore, they are themselves so cold in their love and so coarse in their lives, that they give offence rather than make others better, and thus they make the arrows of God dull and powerless.

"The fifth verse laments, and shows how it goes with such preachers, namely, that few of their hearers believe the gospel, and they but cast it to the wind. This pains the Spirit, who so greatly desires that every one may receive it with joy. Therefore he says: 'Ah, woe is me! Ah, my sorrow! I must so long here wander as a stranger, for I do not find the kingdom of God among them. And they will not enter it. I have preached so long and it does no good. They still remain as they are, and I must also live among them, and dwell in the tents of Kedar.' Kedar is the name given in the Hebrew language to Arabia, and means sad or gloomy, like persons who are mourning. The Arabians are a wild, savage, insolent, uncultivated people. Hence he here calls those who are not obedient to the gospel Kedar, because they will not suffer themselves to be chastened by the gospel.

"The sixth verse shows that he is not alone despised, but also persecuted for the sake of the Word, and must yet remain among these evil men. 'They hate peace,' says he, i. e., the divine peace, which we enjoy when we have within peace with God in a good conscience, and without peace with all men, injuring no one, but doing good to all. They hate peace, for they persecute the Word, which teaches and brings such peace; and they defend their teaching, which makes evil consciences before God through works of unbelief, giving rise to sects and strife in many forms among the people.

"The seventh verse gives answer, and presents its defence, against the false charges which the ungodly bring against true Christians. For they say that such doctrine is seditious and causes contentions in the world. To this he says: 'It is not my fault, for I kept the peace, injured no one, except that I preached about the true peace; that they could not endure, and began to stir up strife, and persecuted me.' Just so Elijah had to hear from King Ahab the charge that he had made Israel to sin, although, as Elijah replied, it was Ahab himself, and not he, who made Israel to sin.

"You see here, dear Friends, that your case is at the same time described, and it happens to you just as is written in this Psalm. You must bear the name of being seditious, although you have done nothing but hear and speak and spread abroad the Word of God. Because of this, the temple-slaves and soul-hunters at Mentz have stirred up strife on your account, and have hated and persecuted the peace which you taught, and yet you must continue to dwell and must wander long among such enemies of peace for God's sake, and must be strange and badly-treated guests in the tents of Kedar.

"Now what will you do? Avenge yourselves, you cannot; and if you could, it would not be proper. Nor will it do to wish them evil, for Christ says (Matt. v. 44): 'Bless them that curse you, and pray for them that despitefully use you and persecute you.' What shall you do then? Nothing better than to turn your eyes away from the men who injure you, and look upon the knave who owns and drives them, and consider how you may take revenge and wreak your passion upon him. But he has neither flesh nor bone, he is a spirit. Therefore, as St. Paul says, you have not to fight with flesh and blood, but with spiritual knaves in the air ('spiritual wickedness in high places') with the rulers of the blind, dark world. What else could the miserable whoremongers and gluttons at Mentz do? They have to do just what their god, the devil, drives them to; they are not their own masters, and we ought therefore most heartily to pity them. They profess to be maintaining Christian doctrine, and yet live more shamefully than adulterers and prostitutes; as though the Holy Spirit could effect anything for his honor through such tools of the devil, unless indeed he should do so without their knowledge or consent, as in the cases of Judas, Caiaphas and Pilate.

"There is, therefore, only one course left, namely, that you, as this Psalm directs, cling to the Lord in this distress, call upon him to protect you against such evil tongues, and pray earnestly and with the whole heart for strong archers, who may shoot sharp arrows at the devils, never missing aim, and for fiery coals of juniper, who with burning zeal may enkindle the misguided, blind multitude, and by a pure life enlighten them to the glory and praise of God's name. If you will but do this, you will soon be so richly avenged upon the devil and his scales, that your hearts will be filled with rejoicing. But be sure to present such petitions with all confidence, and do not doubt that God, for the sake of whose Word you are tormented, will hear you and send out his arrows and coals in great numbers, so that, when they shall have suppressed the Word in one place in Miltenberg, it may break out in ten other places, and that, the more they blow upon the fire, the more hotly it may burn.

"That the Word of God does not yet make such progress as it rightfully should, and as we would gladly see (although they think that its progress is altogether too rapid), can be laid only to our own account, because we are too indolent to pray for sharp arrows and hot coals. He has commanded us to pray that his kingdom may come and his name be hallowed, i. e., that his Word and Christians may increase and become strong; but, because we allow everything to remain as it is, and do not pray with earnestness, the cause moves on so slowly, the arrows are blunt and powerless, the coals are cold and crude, and the devil is not yet very much afraid of us.

"Therefore let us wake up and be active, for it is time. The devil is playing us many an evil game on every hand; let us therefore for once show him something that will sorely vex him, and avenge ourselves; that is, let us pray to God without ceasing, until he send us trained archers with sharp arrows and plenty of coals.

"See now, my dear Masters and Friends, I have

ventured thus to write you a letter of consolation, although others could have done it better and have more cause than I. But since my name is also mixed up in the matter, and you are persecuted as being Lutherans, it was not unseemly for me, I think, to concern myself in your behalf as well as in my own.

"And although I do not like it, that the doctrine and those who maintain it are called Lutheran, but have to endure from them that they thus dishonor the Word of God by attaching my name to it; yet they must allow Luther, the Lutheran doctrine and the Lutheran people, to remain and be exalted in honor. They and their doctrine, on the other hand, shall perish and be put to shame, even though the whole world should mourn and all the devils be sorely vexed. If we continue to live, they can have no peace on our account; if we die, they can still less have peace. In fine, they cannot get rid of us unless they come down and willingly surrender to us, and all their wrath and raging cannot help them. For we know whose Word it is that we preach, and the whole of them together cannot take it from us. This is my prophecy, and it shall not fail. May God have mercy upon them!

"I hereby commend you, dear Friends, to the grace and mercy of God, and do you also pray to

God for me, poor sinner; and may his blessing rest upon all your preachers, who preach Christ and not the Pope nor the temple-apprentices at Mentz. The grace of God be with you. Amen."

It was in this way only that Luther could manifest his interest in the adherents of the gospel far away from the Elbe, on the Lech and the Main, expressing to them his deepest sympathy and giving them most wholesome counsels, to enable them to bear their grievous afflictions in patience and with joy, to the honor of God and the glory of his name. He came to the assistance of those who in his own more immediate neighborhood were called upon to endure all manner of hostility and persecutions, by writing to them similar letters of consolation, as, for example, to the Christians chased out of Oschatz by Duke George, whose distress had been reported to him by a woman of Daum;* to the adherents of the gospel driven out of Leipzig,† and to the sorely-pressed good people of Mitweida, of whom Antonius Lauterbach, preacher in the electoral Leisnig, had notified him.‡ But he also carried through their appeals to

* Briefe. De Wette, 4, 433 f. (January 20. 1533.)
† Ibid., 4, 463. Werke, Jena. 6, 6 ff. (June or July, 1533).
‡ Briefe. De Wette, 4, 609 (June 27, 1535).

the strict civil rulers, as that of those who had been driven out of Leipzig, on account of the Gospel;* gave them advice in all manner of questions of conscience, as to others, also of Leipzig, who were to be compelled to receive the communion in but one element;† welcomed them kindly to Wittenberg; consulted patiently and fully with them; and, when his physical condition did not permit him to ascend the pulpit in the city church, preached the Gospel to them in his own house, as *e. g.*, on Whit-monday, 1534, to the faithful confessors who had been driven out of Leipzig.‡

As, furthermore, the spiritual adviser must, even in worldly affairs, not give counsel only, but must render personal, practical assistance, if the forlorn one cannot help himself, or if his own effort has no prospect of success; so the Reformer at all times endeavored to do all in his power to assist those who had been despoiled of their property in regaining possession of it. It was thus that he interceded with his gracious lord, the Elector John, December 16th, 1527,§ for a certain Simon Manne-

---

*Briefe. De Wette, 4, 405 and 6, 135 (Oct. 4, 1532).

†Ibid., 4, 443 and 6, 141 (April 11, 1533).

‡Comp. Marginal note to this sermon in Hauspostille, Nürnberg, 1545.

§ Briefe. De Wette, 3, 247 f.

witz, who had, for the sake of gospel, been oppressed and robbed of his paternal inheritance by the Bishop of Meissen, representing that the little property of the poor man was included in the Würzburg district under the protection of the Elector.

It was known how willingly Luther always helped the oppressed and the forlorn, and how much a word from him availed. He was therefore overrun with applications, not alone from such as desired to secure an investigation by some person of high rank or some wise city council, but also from such as thought that they were unjustly treated by those in authority. George Schmidt, for example, spreads before him, with the most solemn asseverations of his own innocence, his trouble, *i. e.*, that the council of Magdeburg had done him injustice, and Luther at once appeals to Nicholas Amsdorf, his confidential friend at that place.* A certain poor man leaves him no rest, although he cannot by the utmost exertion render him any assistance; finally, he humbly entreats the Elector "to advance his cause by a short letter to the authorities of Jessen." † Then comes a poor fisherman who had at one time fished in forbidden waters, and of whom

* Briefe. De Wette, 3, 86 (January 7, 1526).
† Ibid., 3, 101 (April 14, 1526).

the officer of the law demands ten silver schocks in penalty. Luther requests Spalatin* to effect a modification of the punishment. "I do not ask," writes he, "that he be not punished as an example to promote reverence for lawful authority, but that the punishment may be such as not to extort from him all his living. I would throw him into prison for a few days, or let him live on bread and water for a week, so that every one might see the object of the penalty to be not destruction, but amendment." Rents are withheld in Henneberg territory from a relative of the Reformer, Werner Bergk of Salzungen, "on account of some purchased bell-metal."† An Eisenach citizen, Caspar Schalbe, is denied the possession of his property, because a servant girl has circulated evil reports about him.‡ A preacher of the Gospel, Amandus by name, has been placed in custody, as a seditious man, by Duke George of Pomerania, although the city of Stettin, and the preachers there, had given him the best of testimonials.§ A preacher in Electoral Saxony has been arrested, because he has expressed an imprudent opinion in matters relating

---

*Briefe. De Wette, 2, 206 (June 7, 1522.)
† Ibid., 3, 184 (June 16, 1527).
‡ Ibid., 3 (119), 162 (March 1, 1527).
§ Ibid., 3, 107 f. (April 26, 1526).

7

to marriage.* These cases are all referred to Luther, and the dear man of God, unable himself to help, grasps his pen, and implores his Elector John to look into them.

We know how grievously Carlstadt had provoked him; but this does not prevent him from speaking a good word in behalf of the latter to his gracious lord, and requesting that he, who was said to be unsettled at Orlamund, being under very strong suspicion of complicity in the Peasant War, might come to Kemberg and live in peace.†

The Peasants, too, had done much to make life truly bitter for him: none the less on that account, he requests the Elector graciously to assist a poor man, Michael Koch, a citizen of Mühlhausen, to recover his property, since he had been already long enough driven about in misery. "Since many others," we read in this letter,‡ "who also took part in the insurrection have received permission to return and have been admitted; he begs that he, too, may for God's sake be admitted, and he makes the very best and strongest promises that he knows how to make." "I pray your Electoral Grace to look upon his misery, and let him

* Briefe. De Wette, 3, 242 (Dec. 2, 1527).
† Ibid., 3, 28 and 137 (Sept. 12, 1525, and Nov. 22, 1526).
‡ Ibid., 3, 168 (Apr. 28, 1527).

have the benefit of my intercession as far as may be proper, for I greatly pity the poor man."

His love toward the forlorn is so strong, that he restrains his wrath against the Elector Albrecht of Mentz, and speaks a good word to him in behalf of Asmus Günthel, the son of a citizen of Eisleben, who had been found eating and drinking with the Peasants in certain outworks that were taken by storm. "May your Electoral Grace," says he in his appeal,* "consider that this insurrection has been quelled, not by human hand or counsel, but through the grace of God, who has had compassion upon us all and especially upon those in authority. May you also in turn deal graciously and mercifully with the poor people, as indeed well becomes spiritual rulers, and as is more fitting in them than in worldly rulers, in order that the grace of God may be recognized and acknowledged with thankfulness, and that they may prove before the world that they have not desired and sought their own pleasure. There are, alas, far too many others who treat the people with such cruelty, and conduct themselves with such ingratitude toward God, as though they would wantonly awaken again and bring upon themselves the wrath and displeasure of God and of the people, to cause a

*Briefe. De Wette, 3, 16 (July 21, 1525).

new and worse insurrection. God can soon have another one prepared, in order that they who have shown no mercy may perish without mercy."

That Luther repelled no one in forlorn circumstances, is strikingly illustrated by his efforts in behalf of the violent Hans Kohlhase. The splendid horses of the latter were siezed as stolen property by an electoral nobleman, Günther of Zaschwitz, and so abused, that by the time his title was clearly proved, they were worth nothing. Kohlhase demanded damages, but the squire paid no attention to his claim. The Elector of Brandenburg interested himself in the cause of his subject; the Elector of Saxony promised to assist the poor man in securing his rights: but the electoral officers were unwilling to bring action against their associate and occasioned unreasonable delay. Unfortunately, the injured man undertook to help himself, and robbed, burnt* and murdered throughout Saxony to such an extent as to terrorize the country. "Luther, blessed man," so reports a manuscript district chronicle of Peter Hafftitius,†

---

* We learn from Luther's letters, that he burnt down Schlieben (De Wette, 5, 158, February 2, 1539), and Marzahna (Ibid., 5, 272, March 5, 1540) and plundered a miller (Ibid., 5, 170, March 2, 1539).

† Schöttgen, Diplomatische und curieuse Nachlese der Historie von Ober-Sachsen, 3, 535 f.

"weighing and taking to heart all the circumstances, and anxious to avoid further trouble which might result for both parties, wrote to Kohlhase and warned him to desist from his depredations, and sought to impress upon him by every consideration what the result would be for himself, and how God would surely, if he would not give him due honor and leave vengeance to him, bring to light and avenge the outrages. Kohlhase thereupon, unobserved, rode off with one companion to Wittenberg, took lodging at the inn, and in the evening, leaving his servant there, he approached Dr. Luther's door, knocked, and announced that he wished to speak with the Doctor. After the Doctor had several times through his servant requested him to give his name and state his errand, and he had refused to do this and yet strenuously insisted that he must speak with the Doctor in person, it occurred to the latter that it might be Kohlhase. He therefore went to the door himself, and said: 'Is it you, Hans Kohlhase?' to which the visitor replied: 'Yes, honored Doctor.' He then admitted him, conducted him secretly to his own chamber, and sent for Philip (Melanchthon), Cruciger, Major, and other theologians. Kohlhase then reported the whole transaction to them, and they remained with him until late in the night.

Early in the morning he made confession before the Doctor, received the holy sacrament, and promised them that he would cease his depredations and inflict no injury in the future upon Saxon territory, a promise which was never broken. He then departed from the inn unrecognized and unobserved, they having given him assurance that they would help to advance his cause." This was unfortunately not to be accomplished so easily nor quickly. Kohlhase became impatient, and met his fate.

CHAPTER IV.

HOW LUTHER ADMONISHED THE ERRING.

THROUGHOUT his entire life, the Reformer was, to a most extraordinary extent, brought into contact with people who cherished erroneous opinions, or whose consciences were perverted, especially with people who, unable to find the right way, wandered about in uncertainty or had actually started upon some course that was utterly wrong.

The very act, indeed, by which he began his reformatory activity was an admonition of the erring! We are accustomed to regard the nailing of the ninety-five theses on indulgences upon the door of the castle-church at Wittenberg, which occurred at noon on the ever-memorable 31st of October, 1517, as the first act of faith on the part of the Reformer.

This can hardly be considered as strictly accurate. Luther did not set himself up as a Reformer. He was, in the ordering of Providence, driven further step by step by the assaults of his enemies, and led into an ever deeper knowledge of the truth. What he in his ninety-five theses proclaimed to the learned world, he had already taught in the confessional at Wittenberg. He had been compelled to teach thus, that he might not make himself a partaker of other men's sins, and suffer those entrusted to his care, misled by soul-destroying error, to rush blindly into the pit of destruction.

Let us hear what a friend and contemporary of Luther, the above-mentioned Myconius, truthfully reports:* "In the year 1517, certain persons came to Dr. Martinus at Wittenberg with purchased indulgence papers, and, relying upon the grace which these assured, made confession before him. As they boldly confessed to the gravest offences, and declared that they had no intention of forsaking their adultery, usury, fornication, robbery, and such other sins and wickedness, the Doctor refused to absolve them, on the ground that they manifested no true penitence nor amendment. They then appealed to their papal letters, and to the grace and indulgence granted by Tetzel. Martinus adhered to his decision, appealing to the passage: 'Except ye repent, ye shall all likewise

---

*Myconius, Hist. Reformationis von Cyprian, 1718, p. 21. Teutzel, Monatl. Unterredungen, 1697, p. 902. Vogel, Tetzel, 276.

perish' (Lk. xiii. 5). As he would not absolve them, they returned to Tetzel, and complained to him that this Augustinian monk would pay no regard to their letters. Tetzel was at Jüterbog, which place was at that time under the jurisdiction of the Archbishop of Magdeburg. When the news was brought to him, he became very angry, raging, scolding, and terribly cursing the pulpit, threatening to bring all manner of evil upon the arch-heretics, as he called the preaching-monks of the day. In order to terrify the people, he had a fire kindled in the market-place several times in the week, and announced that he had instructions from the Pope thus to burn the heretics, who opposed the most holy father, the Pope, and his most holy indulgences."

That Luther, when he refused in the confessional to have anything to do with the indulgence-business, and when he, in consequence of the assaults which had been made upon him by the preacher of indulgences, Tetzel, made open declaration of his principles in the ninety-five theses, thereby placed his position and his life in jeopardy, is a universally acknowledged fact. This he well knew; but he knew also that no portion of the pure, true doctrine dare be surrendered, and that it was his duty, as a doctor of theology, pledged by oath to the Holy Scriptures, to venture everything in maintaining and defending the Word of God, and that he was under obligation, still further, as an ordained priest and regularly-called spiritual adviser, to admonish the erring who had been led astray into grievous error. The Reformer had a conscience, and the Reformation was the achievement of a good conscience opposing the conscienceless forgiveness of sins.

Luther's entire reformatory activity may be regarded from a single point of view, *i. e.*, as an admonition of the erring. He pointed the erring to the one Mediator between God and men, who alone has power to forgive sins and to help from death to life. He pointed the erring, who had been driven to leaking fountains in the wilderness, and lay there languishing, to the fountain of Holy Scripture, and taught them with the hand of faith to draw from it and to drink the water of life. But it is not our purpose to dwell upon this reformatory activity, whose object was the salvation of souls in the congregation through public preaching. The care of souls, of which we now speak, has to do with single persons. The great Reformer, in his concern for all Christendom and for the many evangelical congregations in whose behalf he exerted himself, never lost from view the individual soul. Nor did he wait until he was applied to for spiritual counsel, which occurred in countless instances and cost him a vast amount of effort and labor; but, wherever he found occasion and opportunity, he laid hold with a firm, skillful and decisive hand. He had a clear eye, and it was turned alike upon high and low. He approached high lords and common people without distinction, and, if they were in error, did not hesitate to admonish them.

Count Albrecht, of Mansfeld, is a personality not entirely unknown in Reformation history. He was the first in Thuringia to cope successfully with the insurgent peasants, surprising them at Osterhausen, and had already in 1518 attached himself with such decision to the new doctrine, that he sent Luther warning, through the well-known Augustinian prior, Johann Lange, of the plots of certain influential men against him.* In the course of time, however, the Count fell into wrong ways. He began to cherish doctrinal errors, and to repudiate utterly the obligations of brotherly love. Luther observed this with deep regret, and admonished his "gracious and heartily beloved liege-lord, the noble, high-born Lord Albrecht, Count of Mansfeld," in the following letter :†

* Briefe. De Wette, 1, 129.
† Ibid., 5, 512 ff.

"Grace and Peace in the Lord, and my poor Pater-noster. Gracious Lord, I beg most earnestly that your Reverend Grace may accept this writing of mine in a Christian and gracious spirit. Your Reverend Grace knows that I am a child of the sovereignty of Mansfeld, and have to the present day cherished natural affection for my Fatherland, as even the books of all heathen nations declare that every child has a natural affection for his fatherland. Besides this, God accomplished in the beginning of the Gospel so many praiseworthy achievements through your Reverend Grace, so excellently ordering the affairs of churches, pulpits and schools for the praise and glory of God, and made your Reverend Grace so eminently and gloriously useful in quelling the insurrection of the peasants, that I, for such and other reasons, cannot so easily forget nor omit from my cares and prayers your Reverend Grace.

"But it comes to my ears, chiefly through many rumors and complaints, that your Reverend Grace is said to have fallen away from the course first entered upon and to have become quite different, which, as I think your Reverend Grace will readily believe, if it were true, would cause me heartfelt sorrow for your Reverend Grace. For now people will talk against the Christian faith, and say, as I have myself often heard: 'What need of the Gospel? That which is fore-ordained must come to pass. Let us do what we will. If we are to be saved, we will be saved, etc.' This is now thought to be great shrewdness and wisdom, although we theologians knew it long ago and also God himself. Should your Reverend Grace be entangled in these thoughts and temptations, it would cause me heartfelt sorrow, for I was once myself entangled in them, and had not Dr. Staupitz, or, rather, God through Dr. Staupitz, helped me out, I would have been drowned in them and would have been in hell long ago. For such diabolical thoughts finally drive the timid-hearted to despondency, despairing of the grace of God; whilst those who are bold and courageous become despisers and enemies of God, and say: 'Let things go as they will! I will do as I please. I'm lost anyhow.'

"How I wish that I could speak with your Reverend Grace face to face, for I am grieved beyond measure for the soul of your Reverend Grace, since I cannot esteem your Reverend Grace so lightly as the reprobate Henry's and Mentz's.*

---

* "Heinzen und Meinzen." By the former of these terms we are to understand Henry VIII. King of England and Henry, Duke of Brunswick; by the latter, without doubt, the Elector Albrecht of Mentz, and perhaps others.

One cannot talk so well to another with the pen. Nevertheless—to write briefly of this matter, my Gracious Lord—it is true, that what God has decreed must certainly come to pass; otherwise he would be a liar in his promises, upon which we must place our faith or shamefully fail, and that is impossible. But here is, at the same time, this great difference to be observed, namely: What God has revealed to us, promised or commanded, that we are to believe, and to act accordingly, assured that he will not lie: but what he has not revealed to us, nor promised, that we are not to and cannot know, much less can we act accordingly. Whoever troubles himself much about this, is tempting God, since he neglects that which he is commanded to know and to do, and concerns himself about that which he is not commanded to know and to do. This can only produce people who ask not for God's Word and sacrament, but give themselves up to wild living, mammon, tyranny, and every kind of dissolute life. For, with such thoughts, they can have no faith, nor hope, nor love to man or to God, whom they despise, because they are not permitted to know what he secretly thinks; although he has so abundantly revealed himself in everything that can minister to their benefit or salvation, from which they wantonly turn away. No man would tolerate a servant, who should refuse to perform his appointed duty, unless he knew in advance all the secret thoughts of his master in regard to all his possessions. And shall God not have power likewise to have some secrets to himself, beyond that which he has commanded us?

"Let your Reverend Grace only think how it would be, if we were to be guided by such thoughts of the secret judgments of God, for example: 'Why does he permit his Son to become man? Why does he establish family relations — fatherhood and motherhood? Why does he ordain civil law and government? What more is needed? That which is to happen, will happen without all this! What need is there of the devil, the Holy Scriptures, and all created things? What he wishes to do, he can do without any of these.' But we are told that he desires to accomplish his purpose, as far as now revealed, through us as fellow-laborers, 1 Cor. iii. 9: therefore we should let him manage and not trouble ourselves about it, but do that which he has commanded us. Thus also says Solomon, Prov. xxv.: 'He that would search out royalty shall be crushed;'* and Sirach iii. (vs. 22 and 23): 'Understand not what is too high, but

---

* Verse 27, according to the Vulgate, or old Latin version.

think what is commanded thee;' and when the disciples asked the Lord whether he would at that time establish the kingdom of Israel, he replied: 'It is not for you to know the time or the hour, which my Father hath kept in his own power, but go ye and be my witnesses.' (Acts i. 7 and 8.) As though he should say: Let my Father and me see to the events of the future; go ye and do what I command you.

"Accordingly, I beseech your Reverend Grace most earnestly not to forsake the Word and sacrament, for the devil is an evil spirit, far too cunning for your Reverend Grace, as likewise for all saints, to say nothing of all men; as I myself also discover, although I am scarcely ever off my guard for a single day. Men so easily become cold, and their indifference grows ever greater: and if there were no other result of the devil's cunning, this would be reason enough to bid him flee without a moment's delay, and let the heart be warmed again. Thus, doubtless, your Reverend Grace himself feels that he is already cold and gone astray after mammon, aiming to become very rich, and also, according to common complaints, pressing his subjects altogether too severely and sharply, thinking to take them from their ancestral homes and possessions, and almost to make them his own property—which God will not endure, or, enduring, will bring the earldom to abject poverty. It is his gift, and he can easily take it away again, and that without recompense, as Haggai says (i. 6): 'Ye gather much, but ye put it into a bag with holes, and the Lord bloweth upon your grain till there is nothing left.'

"I have heard it said that some propose to introduce in Germany a form of government like that of France. Well, if they would stop first to ask whether that would be right and well-pleasing to God, I would not object. Let it be considered, too, that the kingdom of France, which was once a golden, glorious kingdom, is now so impoverished in both property and people, that it has become, instead of a golden, a leaden kingdom, and that, although formerly far-famed as the Christian kingdom, it has formed an alliance with the Turks. That is the way it goes when God and his Word are despised.

"I write thus candidly to encourage your Reverend Grace, for I am now much nearer to my grave than people think; and I beg, as before, that your Reverend Grace may deal more mildly and graciously with the subjects of your Reverend Grace, and allow them to remain; then shall your Reverend Grace also remain, by the blessing of

God, both here and in the life to come.* Otherwise, you shall lose both worlds, and be like the man in Æsop's fable, who opened the goose that laid every day a golden egg, and thereby lost the golden eggs and the goose that laid them, or like the dog in Æsop, that lost the piece of meat by snapping at its reflection in the water: for it is most certainly true, as Solomon in so many of his proverbs says, that he who wants too much gets least of all.

"To conclude, I am concerned for the soul of your Reverend Grace, which I cannot bear to have cast out of my cares and prayers, for that would to me mean, just as truly, cast out of the Church. I have been compelled to write, not only by the commandment of Christian love, but also by the severe threatening which God has announced to us in the third chapter of Ezekiel, namely, that we shall be condemned for others' sins. He says (verse 18): 'If thou tell not the sinner of his sin, and he die therein, I will require his soul at thy hands,' for to this end have I made thee a guardian of souls.

"I trust your Reverend Grace will therefore receive kindly this exhortation, for I cannot allow myself to be condemned for the sin of your Rev-

---

* Compare, for Albrecht's views, Briefe. De Wette, 5, 287.

erend Grace, but must on the contrary make every possible effort, that your Reverend Grace may with me be saved. Thus I shall at least be guiltless before God. I commend you to the abounding grace and mercy of God.

"Your Reverend Grace's willing and true-hearted,
"MARTINUS LUTHER, D.
"*Day of the Innocents, in the year 1542.*"

The interest which Luther manifested in the forlorn Hans Kohlhase has been mentioned in the preceding chapter. Hafftitius informs us that he also sent a warning to the depredating horseman. There is found in Luther's works a letter addressed to some unknown person, warning against the taking of revenge. De Wette reports* that, according to a marginal note in a certain Wolfenbüttel codex, this letter was addressed to Kohlhase, which may very well have been the case. It runs thus:

"Grace and Peace in Christ. My good Friend. I have been truly grieved, and yet grieve, as God knows, over your misfortune. It would have been better in the first place not to have undertaken revenge, since it cannot be undertaken without a burdening of the conscience; for a private vengeance is forbidden by God, Deut. xxxii.

* Briefe, 4, 567.

35, Rom. xii. 19: 'Vengeance is mine, saith the Lord, I will repay,' etc, and it cannot be otherwise than that he who enters upon it shall run the risk of doing much against God and man which a Christian conscience cannot approve.

"It is true, indeed, that your injury and disgrace must give you pain, and that you are bound to redeem and maintain your honor, but not by sins or wrong-doing. Do what is right in the right way, says Moses: one wrong cannot right another. Now to make one's self a judge and execute judgment upon others is certainly wrong, and the wrath of God will not suffer it to go unpunished. What you can lawfully accomplish, it is right to do; but if you cannot thus secure your rights, then there is no other way but to suffer wrong. God, who permits you to suffer wrong, has assuredly some reason for it. He does not mean thereby to injure you, but can fully recompense you in some other way. Do not therefore be discouraged.

"And what would you do, if he should yet further afflict—in wife, child, body and life? Nevertheless, you would still have to say, if you would be a Christian: 'My dear Lord God, I have well deserved it; thou art just, and thy punishment is altogether too light in proportion to my sins. And what is all our suffering, compared with the suffering of his Son, our Lord Jesus Christ?

"Accordingly, if, as you write, you desire my advice, it is this: Accept terms of peace wherever they can be obtained, and rather suffer injury in possessions and honor, than prosecute further an undertaking in which you must make yourself responsible for the sins and villainy of all who may follow your fortunes. They are, at any rate, not to be depended on; they have no true love for you, but are seeking gain for themselves. They will at length betray you, and you will then have the worst of the game. Don't paint the devil over your door, nor invite him to enter as a sponsor. He will come at any rate. Such companions are the devil's house-servants, and their end is commonly in accordance with their deeds.

"But you ought to consider what a grievous burden your conscience will have to carry if you knowingly bring ruin upon so many people, as you have no right to do. Be contented, for the glory of God regard your injury as inflicted by him, and for his sake endure it meekly. You will then see that he will bless you again, and so richly reward your labor that you will highly prize the patience which you have shown. To this may you be helped by Christ, our Lord, the teacher and pattern of all patience, and the helper in distress. Amen.

"*Tuesday after St. Nicholas' Day (Dec. 8), 1534.*"

Count Albrecht took to heart the admonition of Luther, and died in peace in a good old age; but Kohlhase, unfortunately, rejected the counsel of the spiritual adviser, and followed instead the advice of his comrade, George Nagelschmied, which brought him to the gallows.

It could not be otherwise, but that just at the time of the Reformation the deepest interest should be aroused by the question, whether the princes of Germany had authority to take up arms against the Emperor; for Charles V. in various ways threatened and attempted to suppress by force the preaching of the Gospel, and to crush the evangelical church. Luther was, in consequence, applied to for his faithful counsel by many who could not decide for themselves, and knew not what course to pursue. He gives expression to his sound views upon this question in a short letter to Wenzel Link, pastor at Nuremberg :*

"As you have just written and requested that we report to you whether it is true, as was written to you, that we have given counsel that the Em-

---

* Briefe. De Wette, 6, 127, and 4, 212.

peror may be resisted, I assure you in response that we have in no way given such counsel. But, as some were declaring that theologians have nothing to do with these things, and that they should not be consulted nor concern themselves about them, but the jurists, who say we may defend ourselves, I said for my own self : 'As a theologian, I do not advise it; but, if the jurists can show and prove from their laws that it is right, they may see to that and bear the responsibility. For if the Emperor has appointed in his law that he may be in this case resisted, let him then be satisfied and submit to the law which he has given and appointed or confirmed and approved ; yet I do not counsel nor give judgment in regard to this law which allows and permits self-defence, but I stick to my theology. I cheerfully acknowledge, and make no secret of it, that a prince or ruler is a worldly person, and therefore that which he does befitting a government, and in accordance with the laws, he does not as a Christian ; for a Christian is not a prince, nor government, nor vassal, nor any personage in the world. Whether now a government, as a government, may resist the Emperor and protect itself and its subjects from unjust violence, of that they may judge. I let them decide and answer to their consciences. It certainly is not befitting a

Christian, as one who has died to the world, and has nothing at all to do with worldly affairs, nor concerns himself about them.'

"So far has the matter gone, and you may report this to Herr Lazarus* as my opinion and sentiment, although I see very clearly, that, however we may oppose it with all our powers, and cry aloud, they have so thoroughly made up their minds, determined and resolved, that they will certainly defend themselves, and not suffer themselves to be driven or beaten. I may preach and say what I will, it is all in vain. God will be with us, and help, that there may be no occasion for resistance, for he is most certainly upon our side. Of this we have clear proof, for he has brought to naught the decisions of this Diet, so that they have thus far undertaken nothing against us; and he will do likewise in the future. But not all men have faith. I take comfort to myself in this, that, though they will not follow our advice, they will sin the less and act less rashly, if they plan their undertakings in accordance with written imperial laws, and if in so doing they fully believe that they are doing nothing contrary to the Scriptures and God's Word, because they undertake and do

---

* Without doubt, the excellent city clerk of Nuremberg, Lazarus Spengler.

nothing contrary to written law. So I let them go; I am free.
December, 1530".

Luther steadfastly maintained the principle: "A Christian should not resist, but suffer everything, and not take refuge in the pretext, 'it is allowable to repel violence with violence.'"* But he does not forget to add: "If, however, the laws of the jurists permit a Christian, not as a Christian, but as a citizen or member of a civil community, to resist, to that we do not object." †

An error growing out of the canonical laws threatened at that time in the most alarming way the very foundations of domestic life. We refer to the endorsement of secret betrothals. It was very common for young people to become engaged without the knowledge of their parents, and such engagements, which most deeply undermined parental authority and turned into derision all filial regard for father and mother, were acknowledged as binding, and as really equivalent to legal marriage. The Reformer regarded these secret betrothals with abhorrence. He stood here like a wall of brass, which, whenever accidentally struck,

---

* Briefe. De Wette, 4, 233.
† Ibid.

gives forth a loud, clear and long-reverberating tone. That Luther in this matter was far in advance of his time, is proved especially by the powerful letter which he addressed to the consistory at Wittenberg in January, 1544.* How he, as a faithful spiritual adviser, admonishes the erring consistory, of which his own beloved Bugenhagen was a member!

"In the first place," he observes, "I should very gladly have been spared the unpleasant duty, but since I could not reconcile my conscience, as a spiritual adviser in this church, to the decision of the consistory, I have been compelled on account of my office to oppose it. Although I might have overlooked the sin committed both in the betrothals themselves and in their confirmation, involving so much lying and perjury, and such suspicious practices, that it seems, alas, impossible for any one to obtain justice without much injustice and sin (not to speak of the injury and injustice caused by delays, the course of litigation seeming to have no end, and it having become dangerous to be an honest jurist), yet I should have been compelled to speak, because the decision referred to tends to confuse and perplex consciences.

"But the second and chief reason for my opposi-

---

* Briefe. De Wette, 4, 233.

tion is that the whole business, namely, the secret betrothals of both parties, together with their confirmation and the decision of the consistory, is nothing but a cunning piece of the devil's machinery, so constructed that through it the miserable Pope with his abominations of desolation may again sit in our church, and become at length worse than before he was driven out. Surely it was time for me to wake up and look into the matter. For, inasmuch as our consistory knew, or at least ought to have known, what evil is being wrought in our church by secret betrothals, it should of right have acted very differently, i. e., it should have condemned secret betrothals, prohibited their confirmation, and should by no means have rendered such a decision as to commend to our poor youth, in an evil and extreme example, such a work of the devil. A secret betrothal cannot be anything else than the devil's business, brought about through the enemy of God and murderer of souls, the Pope, just as Daniel prophesied that the latter would set himself above and against God, and horribly assail every ordinance of God, such as ecclesiastical, civil and domestic government. Thus he has in this matter abolished the fourth commandment of God, permitted and taught children to be disobedient to their parents, to become robbers and steal themselves from their parents by secret betrothal, in which the honor and authority over their children and property given and committed to parents by God is brought to naught. Still further, as was most befitting in him who is the man of sin and the son of perdition, he has praised and rewarded such abominable sin against God and parents as a good and precious work.

"He has thus deeply distressed parents, and has indeed caused some to die of grief, as might very easily have been the case recently with Magister Philip (Melanchthon), whom I had to restrain by force from hastily giving his consent to his son's betrothal, and who, having before been similarly distressed by the betrothal of his daughter, and complained that his children were so wretchedly stolen from him, would now, if he had made a serious mistake in the case of his son, have grieved himself to death.

"Now, since we, by the grace of God through his holy Word, know what secret betrothal is, namely,—a work of the devil; a shameful sin of disobedience against God and earthly parents; a thief and robber so cruel that he wickedly steals, robs and snatches away from me, not only money and property, but my dearest treasure upon earth, my daughter or my son, perhaps the only son or daughter; and, besides, a jailer and murderer of parents—we should, therefore, when it is learned that a secret betrothal has been made, with all our power urge the parties to it to say nothing about it, rebuke them sharply, not allow them to apply to the court, but by all means restore all things to the former condition, and set free and give back to their parents the son and daughter stolen by the betrothal, tear to pieces and condemn the certificate of betrothal, as it is before God accursed and condemned. Thus we shall not need to endure the wretchedness which the devil seeks to bring upon us. We do not need to set fleas in the wool, nor to permit or teach children to be disobedient; as it is, they disobey far more than is agreeable to God or to us.

"A thief who steals ten or twenty florins is hung; but this thief, who steals from me my child and tortures me to death, I must salute as a benefactor and saint, and welcome him to my estate, in which I can no longer find pleasure, in order that thus the iniquity committed against me may be right gloriously rewarded and honored. Thanks to thee, most holy Pope, for thy good doctrine! Thanks, too, are due to those popish jurists, with whom we are so very anxious to associate in the Church of Christ, even whilst they are trying to break down what we build up and to build up what we break down!"

Contending thus strenuously for the power of parents over their children, Luther sought just as earnestly to impress upon the minds of parents that their authority is not unlimited. The son of a widow of Stolberg, Ursula Schneider, had declared his love to a young woman of Wittenberg, and had returned home to secure the consent of his mother. The widow Schneider, who had learned of Luther's approval, did not give, as he had hoped, a favorable answer, and the son accordingly did not return. The Reformer then exhorted the mother to give her consent without delay:* "But since the minx pleases him so greatly, and is of about his own rank, and a good honest child, of honorable parentage, it therefore still seems to me that you ought to be well satisfied, since he has in filial spirit, like Samson, humbled himself and begged for this minx. It will become you now, as a loving mother, to reconcile your will to the situation. For, although we have written† that children should not engage themselves in marriage without the will of their parents, we have, at the same time, also written that parents should not, and cannot with God's approval, compel or hinder their children according to their own pleasure.

---

*Briefe. De Wette, 5, 186 (June 4, 1539). Comp. 2, 511.
† Comp. Von Ehesachen, 1530.

The son should, indeed, bring no daughter to his parents without their consent; but the father, likewise, should force no wife upon his son. They should both have something to say in the matter. Otherwise, the son's wife must become the father's daughter, and owe the latter no thanks."

As Luther thus sought to promote a proper conception of the relations between parents and children, he was equally concerned for the observance of propriety in the marital relation. Although he very often in letters refers in a jocular way to his "Lord Katie," he was not disposed to tolerate the headship of the wife over her husband. This was known to Stephan Roth, town-clerk of Zwickau, who accordingly upon some pretext sent to him his insubordinate wife to have her ideas upon this subject corrected. The woman was too shrewd for him, however, and did not go to Luther. The latter then gave the faint-hearted husband a complete overhauling in the following terms: *

"Grace and Peace in Christ, together with Proper Control over your Wife. Your lady lord and ruler, my Stephan, whose disregard of your authority much displeases me, has not yet come to me. But I am beginning to be angry at you, too, that you should through the weakness of your disposition,

* Briefe. De Wette 3, 302. 6, 93 (Apr. 12, 1528).

which needs to be fortified by Christian obedience, have suffered this dominion to be established, and to become so powerful. It now appears to be your fault that your wife thus takes every advantage of you. Surely, when you observed that the ass was becoming fractious from good feeding, or, in other words, that your wife was taking advantage of your indulgent and yielding disposition and becoming insubordinate, you should have considered that it is a man's duty to obey God rather than his wife, that is, that the authority of the husband, which St. Paul says is the glory of God, dare not be despised by her and trodden under foot. It is enough, that this glory of God should be so far laid aside as to take upon itself the form of a servant: but it is too much, when it is entirely rejected, extinguished and brought to nought. See to it, therefore, that you act like a man, and so bear the infirmity of your wife as not to confirm her in wickedness, nor, by your base servility, dishonor by a most dangerous example the glory of God which has been committed to you. It is easy enough to draw the line between infirmity and wickedness. Infirmity must be borne, but wickedness must be repressed. Infirmity is quite willing to hear and learn, at least once in twelve hours; but wickedness is stiff-necked and stubborn in its resistance. If your wife sees that you regard her wickedness as an infirmity, what wonder if she becomes utterly depraved! You thus of your own fault throw the window wide open for Satan to come in, and mock and irritate and pester you in every way through the poor weaker vessel. You are a sensible man, and may the Lord grant you to understand what I say, and to believe that I have sincerely tried to give the best advice both to yourself and to your wife, and to ward off Satan. Farewell in Christ."

As Luther in this instance admonished an erring friend, so it was his custom, whenever he observed a failing in any one of his friends or brethren, to take a hand in the matter and restore order again. He heard at one time that a good friend of his in Saxony was taking private matters into the pulpit. "A private matter," he writes,* "ought to be passed over in silence and suppressed, and, like a family quarrel, left to wander up and down in its own place. It ought not to be proclaimed from the housetop, which always makes things worse. My advice is: Let it alone, and learn to be patient and keep your mouth shut, that the noble little flower, patience, may be seen. May the God of peace be with you, and your angry feelings will then soon pass away."†

* Briefe. De Wette, 6, 427.
† Ibid., 5, 574 (July 13, 1543).

He does not permit even those of his friends who occupy the most exalted stations to do as they please. To a Spalatin he represents,* that he ought to treat his school-master in a fraternal spirit and not be too unyielding in the maintaining of his rights; and to Justus Jonas,† that it was not very becoming to bring home the second wife so soon after the death of the first.

The Reformer set up and maintained a lofty standard of attainment for the pastors of churches, but he indignantly rebuked and admonished those who made unreasonable demands upon them. To Magister Johann Schreiner, pastor and superintendent at Grimma, he writes somewhat passionately:‡ "Grace and Peace in Christ. My dear Magister and Pastor. Be kind enough to say to the nobility, or whoever they may be, if Spalatin will not do it, that we cannot make pastors just as they would like to have them, and that they ought to thank God that they can have the pure Word spelled for them out of a book, since they in former times, under the Pope, heard nothing but the foul spurtings of the devil, and had to pay dearly enough for them. Who can give to these noble people for

---

* Briefe. De Wette, 5, 574 (July 13, 1543.)

† Ibid., 5, 556 (May 4, 1543).

‡ Ibid., 5, 69 (July 9, 1537). Compare 4, 194.

their begging nothing but Doctor Martius and Magister Philips for pastors? If they will have none but St. Augustines and Jeromes, let them find these for themselves. If a pastor is satisfactory and faithful to his Lord Christ, surely a nobleman, who is perceptibly less exalted than Christ, should also be satisfied. A prince has to be satisfied in his worldly government, if he can find in the whole circle of his nobility three hewn stones, and must be patient with the others, who answer only for filling in. Such matters as this you ought to arrange in your own district, for we, without having this put upon us, are already so overburdened with the affairs of all lands, that we have no rest nor peace. You may show this letter to princes or lords, or to whomsoever you will, for aught I care.''

It appeared that every one who was unable to satisfy his own mind in questions of duty, or feared to reach wrong conclusions, turned with confidence to the Reformer. The papal clergy at Leipzig determined to give to every Easter communicant a coin, by means of which he might certify to the civil authorities that he had properly received the Holy Supper. Many were perplexed, and inquired of Luther whether they dare receive the Holy Sacrament in the one element, or secure the coin in some other way. "Since now," he decides,* "Duke George undertakes to search out even secret matters of conscience, he deserves indeed, as an apostle of the devil, to be deceived in any way that can be devised; for, in making such demands, he has neither right nor justice on his side, but sins against God and the Holy Spirit. But since we must consider, not what other and wicked people do, be they murderers or robbers, but what it is proper for us to suffer and to do, it will in this case be the best course to say boldly, in the face of the murderers and robbers: I will not do it. If you take from me on this account my property and my body, you will be taking them from Another, who will demand restitution to the last drop of blood, as Peter says (Acts x. 42), 'Jesus Christ has been ordained to be a judge of quick and dead.'"

The sister of Jerome Weller, Barbara Lisskirchen,† of Freiberg, inquired through her brother whether she might receive the Holy Sacrament in both elements secretly at home. This he will not and cannot advise: "for after a while," he writes,‡ "every one might wish to receive it in this way,

---

*Briefe. De Wette, 4, 443 and 6, 141 (April 11, 1533).
† Ibid., 6, 543.
‡ Ibid., 4, 596.

and thus the general church and assembly be forsaken and desolate, although it is intended to be a public and common confession. If you can receive it at some other place, as opportunity may offer, and will take the responsibility, since your conscience desires it and is satisfied, you may do it in the name of God, to whom I commend you in my poor prayers."

A good friend at Linz, on the Danube, Sigmund Hangreuter,* requests through Wolfgang Brauer, pastor at Jessen, a decision of the question, whether he might not administer the Lord's Supper to himself and his family. The categorical response to this inquiry is, No; "because he has no such calling nor command, and because, if the tyrannical ecclesiastics, whose duty it is, refuse to administer the sacrament to him and his, he can yet be saved without it by his faith."

A certain member of the nobility comes to him with the question, whether he can with a good conscience be present at the coronation of the bishop in Merseburg. "Since I cannot know," is the reply,† "what is the state of your heart, I can give no counsel in the matter; you must be your own counselor. So far as it is proper for one to

---

*Briefe. De Wette, 5, 38 (Dec. 27, 1536).
† Ibid., 4, 633 (Sept. 19, 1535).

give counsel to another touching external affairs, I have given mine sufficiently in writing and in public declarations, and have thus done my part. Beyond this, I cannot burden myself with the sins, least of all with the secret sins, of other people."

Extremely interesting is the relation of Luther to Dorothea Jörger, a widow residing at Tollet, later at Köppach, in Austria. Already in the first of his twelve letters to her which have reached us, he calls her his "best, faithful friend."* She placed in the Reformer's hands generous contributions for the support of poor, worthy students of theology. At one time, October 24th, 1533, he acknowledges the receipt of 500 guldens.† She sought and received his counsel in all her affairs, told him her troubles, and rested her hope upon him. Thus, desiring to give her daughters a share in the inheritance of her property, she inquired what to do, since the former had some time before signed a disclaimer to the estate. He replies openly and honorably:‡ "My opinion is, that if you can by kindness prevail upon your sons to give their consent, your desire can be carried out; but, if this cannot be accomplished, and your daughters

---

* Briefe. De Wette, 3, 150.

† Ibid., 4, 490.

‡ Ibid., 5, 10 (July 31, 1536).

have already surrendered their claims, it cannot lay any burden upon your conscience if you are unable to secure again for them what they have given away." She even asks of him and secures a memorandum for a Christian form of last will and testament.*

Christoph Jörger, presumably the oldest son of the above-mentioned lady, always regarded the Reformer as his counselor in questions of conscience. He, as an officer at Vienna, had attended the religious services of the Roman Catholics, and had thereby given offence to the adherents of the evangelical doctrines. Luther, applied to for his advice, replied:† "First of all, since you find your conscience burdened in this matter, you can find no better adviser nor doctor than just that very conscience of yours. Why do you wish to live in such a way that your conscience shall be all the while biting and lashing you and leaving you no rest? That would be indeed, as they used to say, to live in a forecourt of hell. Therefore, if your conscience is restless and uncertain in this matter, try by all means to free yourself from this restlessness, for it works against faith, which tends to make the conscience ever more secure and firm. Remain at

---

* Briefe. De Wette, 6, 139 (Jan. 1, 1533).
† Ibid., 6, 355; 4, 659; 5, 612 (Dec. 31, 1543).

home, as before, with the Word, for should you sacrifice with the others in the procession, and do other things of that kind, your conscience would protest against it. To do such things, after you have learned the truth, would be to take your place with those who have denied the truth, as Paul says in Romans xiv. 23: 'He who acts contrary to his conscience is condemned,' or, as his words read, 'Whatsoever cometh not of faith is sin.' All this, and more, you have I trust sufficiently understood from the Scriptures and other books, which instruct and preserve the conscience. Your king is, in such affairs, the devil's servant." Jörger followed this advice and resigned his office, upon which Luther congratulates him under date of April 17th, 1545.*

* Briefe. De Wette, 5, 729.

CHAPTER V.

HOW LUTHER COMFORTED THE MOURNING.

LUTHER was a man of cheerful, joyous piety. "A Christian should be a cheerful man," is a saying of his* which well deserves to be laid to heart by all. He maintained also that every Christian can be cheerful, if he will but consider what he is and what he has. A certain nun, he relates, was accustomed to say to herself, "I am a Christian," and thus banish the evil spirit of sadness and melancholy. "Say likewise to yourself," he exhorts, "though all else be lost, yet I believe that Christ still lives, and I am baptized and am perfectly satisfied with the Gospel; I am therefore no enemy of the sacraments, nor of the Lord himself, but truly believe that he is a Saviour: the devil can bring up nothing against this."†

He could not endure to see any one in sadness, but was impelled to comfort all such with the comfort wherewith he had been comforted by the God

---

*Tischreden. Aurif., 316 a. Först., 3, 123.

† Ibid., 321 a. Först., 3, 138.

of all grace, and thus fill their sorrowing hearts again with joy.

"Grace and Peace in Christ"—thus he writes to Matthias Weller at Freiberg—* "Honorable, kind and dear Friend. Your dear brother tells me that you are greatly troubled in spirit, and tempted to give way to sorrow. He will no doubt tell you what I have said to him. Now, my dear Matthias, do not in this matter depend upon your own thoughts, but hear what other people have to say; for God has given commandment, that one man shall comfort another, and it is his wish, also, that the afflicted shall receive such comfort as his own voice. He says through St. Paul: 'Comfort the faint-hearted' (1 Thes. v. 14), and in Isaiah xl. 8: 'Comfort, comfort ye my people and speak kindly to them,' and elsewhere: 'It is not my will that a man should be sad, but ye shall serve me with cheerfulness, and bring no sacrifice with sadness,' as Moses and the prophets so often and earnestly admonish. He has therefore also commanded that we should not be cumbered with care, but cast our care on him, since he will care for us, as Peter (first epistle, v. 7) teaches from the 55th Psalm (verse 23).

"Since, then, it is God's wish that one comfort

---

* Briefe. De Wette, 4, 556, and 6, 551.

another, and that every one receive the comfort offered; therefore let your thoughts go, and be sure that the devil is using them to worry you, and that they are not your thoughts, but the suggestions of the miserable devil, who cannot endure that we should have a cheerful thought.

"Hear now, therefore, what we say to you in the name of God, namely, that you should be cheerful in Christ, who is your gracious Lord and Deliverer, and let him care for you, as he most assuredly does, even though you do not yet have what you desire. He still lives; place full confidence in him. That will please him, the Scriptures say, as the best sacrifice; for there is no more pleasing and acceptable sacrifice than a cheerful heart, that rejoices in the Lord.

"Therefore, when you feel sad and almost overwhelmed, just say: 'Come, I must play a hymn to our Lord Christ upon the organ, and sing praises to him, for the Scriptures teach me that he delights in cheerful music and song.' Strike the keys with vigor, and sing away until your evil thoughts are gone, as did David and Elisha. If the devil comes again to disturb you with any care or thought of sadness, defend yourself boldly, and say: 'Away with you, devil! I must now sing and play to my Lord Christ.' Thus you must learn to really resist him, and not allow him to put thoughts into your head; for, if you let one in and listen, he will drive in after it ten other thoughts until you are overpowered. There is nothing better, therefore, than right at the first to smite him on the snout. Like that man who, whenever his wife began to pick and bite at him, drew out his flute from his girdle and piped away with all his might, until she was at last tired out and left him in peace; so strike your organ keys, or call in good companions, and sing away until you learn to despise the devil."

But Luther knew full well that persons in sorrow have not always power to exorcise the spirit of sadness, and to draw for themselves the proper comfort from the Word and works of God. He was therefore always, with diligent and sympathizing hand, extending to the sorrowing friendly and inspiring comfort, out of the fountain which ever flowed for him. No trouble seemed to him so trifling, no sorrow so insignificant, as to be unworthy of his ministry of comfort.

We know how little he himself cared for money and property, and yet he does not despise to offer consolation upon the loss of wealth.

"Grace and Peace in the Lord," he writes to some one unknown to us,* "Honorable, discreet

---

* Briefe. De Wette, 5, 473.

and good Friend. Your dear son has informed me that you are greatly worried over the loss of the property which has been taken from you, and that you desire a few words of comfort from me. Now, my dear Friend, I am truly sorry that you are called to bear this burden and sorrow. May Christ, the very best Comforter of all the distressed, comfort you, as he certainly can and will. Amen.

"Remember that you are not the only one whom the devil brings into distress. Job was afflicted, and not only robbed of everything but his skin, but made to suffer terribly in body and spirit: yet God overruled all for good, and he was again richly comforted. Recall what the 55th Psalm (verse 22) teaches: 'Cast thy burden upon the Lord; he will provide for thee,' and St. Peter (first epistle, v. 7), following the above, 'Beloved brethren, cast all your anxious care upon him, for he careth for you.' Although you may suffer pain for a while, he is yet faithful and sure, and will help at the right time, as he says in Psalm l. 15: 'Call upon me in the day of trouble; so will I deliver thee, and thou shalt glorify me,' for he is called in Psalm ix. 9, 'a timely Helper in trouble.'

"What are our sufferings, compared with those which the Son of God innocently and for us endured? Our weakness makes our sufferings heavy and great; they would be lighter if we were stronger. With this I commend you to God.

"*Tuesday after Exaudi, 1542.*"

The theologians and jurists of Saxony at the Diet of Augsburg were filled with anxiety, fearing the very worst, for the enemies of the Gospel were so numerous, so powerful and so insolent. Luther's genial, beloved sponsor, the noble chancellor, Gregory Brück, was the most hopeful man yet among them. With what masterly skill does the Reformer confirm the weak heart of this man, and through him comfort the fearful and sorrowful!

"Grace and Peace in Christ," he begins.* "Estimable, learned, dear Lord and Sponsor. I have now several times written to my most gracious Lord and to our friends. Indeed, I fear that I have written too much, especially to my most gracious Lord, as though I had any doubt that the comfort and grace of God were more abundant and stronger with your Reverend Grace than with me. But I have been instigated to do it by our friends, some of whom are so despondent and anxious, as though God had forgotten us. He cannot forget us, unless he first forget himself, or unless our cause be not his cause and our doctrine not his

* Briefe. De Wette, 4, 127.

Word. But if we are certain of this, and do not doubt that it is his cause and Word, then is our prayer also certainly heard, and help has been decided upon and prepared for us. This cannot fail, for he says (Isa. xlix. 15): 'Can a woman forget her sucking child, that she should not have compassion upon the fruit of her body? And though she should forget it, yet will I not forget thee: behold, I have graven thee upon my hand.'

"I have lately seen two wonderful things. First, as I was looking out of my window, I saw the stars in the sky and the whole beautiful firmament of God; and yet I saw nowhere any pillar set up by the Master to support this firmament. Still, the sky did not fall, and the firmament is yet standing securely. Now there are some who look for such pillars, and would like to lay hold of them and feel them, and because they cannot do this they tremble and go into convulsions, as though the sky would now certainly fall, for no other reason than because they cannot lay hold upon or see the pillars. If they could only grasp these, the sky would certainly stand secure.

"The other wonder which I saw was this: Great, thick clouds were floating over us, so heavy that they might be compared to a great ocean, and yet I saw no foundation upon which they rested or stood, nor any tubs in which they were held. Nevertheless, they did not fall upon us, but greeted us with a threatening countenance, and fled away. When they were past, there shone out that which held them up, as both their support and our roof, the rainbow. Yet this was such a weak, thin, paltry foundation and roof, that it too vanished in the clouds and appeared more like a shadow (or reflection through colored glass) than a powerful foundation, so that one would have cause to fear on account of the foundation as much as on account of the great weight of waters. Nevertheless, it proved to be the fact, that this frail shadow bore up the weight of waters and protected us. Yet there are some who, in their fear, look upon and regard the thick and heavy weight of waters and clouds more than this thin, narrow and light shadow. They would like to feel the strength of this shadow; and, because they cannot do this, they are afraid that the clouds will produce an everlasting deluge.

"I write thus in friendly jest to Your Worship, and yet in all seriousness, for I have learned with special pleasure that Your Worship has, above all others, kept up good courage and a brave heart in this our trial. I had, indeed, hoped that it might be possible to maintain at least civil peace; but

God's thoughts are far above our thoughts, and it is right as it is, for he answers and does 'above that which we ask or understand' (Eph. iii. 20). 'For we know not how we should ask' (Rom. viii. 26). Should he now answer us just as we ask, *i. e.*, that the Emperor might give us peace, then it would perhaps be *beneath* and not *above* that which we understand, and the Emperor would receive the honor, and not God. But now he wishes himself to give us peace, so that he alone may have the honor, which is due to him alone.

"We would not in this despise the Imperial Majesty, but we pray and wish that the Imperial Majesty may undertake nothing against God and the imperial law. But should this occur (God then help us!), we would, nevertheless, as faithful subjects, not believe that the Imperial Majesty did it, but think that some other and tyrannical persons did it under the name of the Imperial Majesty, and we should thus discriminate between the name of the Imperial Majesty and the work of tyrants, just as we discriminate when heretics and liars use the name of God, honoring the name of God while we shun the lies of those who use it. Thus we neither can nor should at all approve nor accept the schemes of tyrants, which they prosecute under the name of the Imperial Majesty.

"But such work as God in his grace has given us to do, he will by his Spirit bless and carry forward, and he will, without forgetting or neglecting, find the way, the time and the place to help us. They have not accomplished, these men of blood, the half of what they had at this time designed, nor are they yet at home, nor where they would like to be. Our rainbow is weak; their clouds are powerful; but at the end it will be seen of what material both are made. May Your Worship take my prattle kindly, and comfort M. Philip and all the others. May Christ also comfort and preserve our most gracious Lords. To him be praise and thanks to eternity. Amen. To his grace I faithfully commend also Your Worship.

"*Loneliness (Coburg), August 5, 1530.*"

It is very remarkable with what skill Luther thus employed the works of God's hand to give courage to the disheartened; but he, above all, delighted in drawing comfort for the sorrowing from the exhaustless fountain of the Holy Scriptures. This he was ready to do whenever misfortune of any kind befell any one of his many acquaintances. Hearing that his friend, Jerome Baumgärtner, had been surprised and taken prisoner while on a journey, by a knight in Franconia, Johann Thomas, of Rosenberg, who in his quarrel with the city of Nuremberg sought thus to avenge himself upon a highly esteemed native of that city, he immediately sat down and wrote to the distressed wife of Baumgärtner:*

"Grace and Peace in our dear Saviour and Lord Jesus Christ. Honorable, virtuous, dear Lady. How deeply my heart is grieved by your sorrow and misfortune, is known to God, who sees and hears my groanings. Every heart, indeed, grieves for the beloved, noble man, that he should be so wickedly held in the hands of the enemies. May God hear our prayers and those of all pious hearts; for it is certain, that all pious hearts are praying fervently for him, and it is certain, also, that such prayers are heard by God and acceptable to him.

"Meanwhile, we must take comfort from the divine promise, repeated so often in the Psalter, that he will not forsake nor forget his people; for we know that your husband is a true man in the faith of Christ, which he has grandly made known and adorned with many noble fruits. It is therefore not possible that God should have cast him off, but, as he has through his holy Word called him to himself and received him to his gracious bosom, so he is now still keeping and will daily and forever

* Briefe. De Wette, 5, 672.

keep him in his bosom. He is yet the same God, who, up to the time of this misfortune, kept him as his own dear Christian and a child of life; and he will still remain for him the same God, even though he for a short time assume a different attitude, to test a little our faith and patience. He has said (John xvi. 20, 22): 'Ye shall weep and lament, but your sorrow shall be turned into joy, which no one shall take from you!' This promise he will keep for us without fail.

"Our sufferings have not yet become so deep and bitter as were those of his own dear Son and of the mother of our Lord. By the thought of these we should be comforted and strengthened in our sufferings, as St. Peter teaches us (first epistle, iii. 18): 'Christ has once suffered for us, the just for the unjust.' Though the devil and his followers now rejoice in our misfortune, they shall yet have to lament bitterly enough, and for their brief joy they shall have long mourning. But we have the great and glorious advantage, that God is gracious and friendly to us, as well as all the angels and the universe, and that, therefore, the misfortunes of these bodies cannot injure our souls, but must, on the contrary, be useful to us, as St. Paul says, Rom. viii. 28: 'We know that all things must work for good to them that love God.' According to the body, it gives us pain, and should and must give us pain, as otherwise we would not be true Christians, suffering with Christ and weeping with those that weep.

"Therefore, my dear Lady, pray and have patience, for you do not suffer alone, but you have many, many noble, faithful, pious hearts, that sympathize most deeply with you, and that are now acting according to the Scripture (Matt. xxv. 36): 'I was in prison and ye came unto me.' Yea, verily, in a great throng we visit the beloved Baumgärtner in his prison, that is, the Lord Christ himself, imprisoned in the person of his faithful member. We pray and call upon God to deliver him, and thus fill you and all of us with rejoicing. May the Lord Jesus himself, who bids us comfort one another, and who also comforts us through his blessed Word, comfort and strengthen your heart through his Spirit in unwavering patience until the blessed end of this and every misfortune. To him, with the Father and the Holy Spirit, be praise and glory forever. Amen.

"MARTINUS LUTHER, D.

"*Tuesday after Visitationis Mariæ (July 7), in the year 1544.*"

Seldom indeed did any one within the circle of

Luther's acquaintances suffer any domestic affliction without receiving from him, either through some other friend or directly in writing, a word of comfort. When we glance at the number of consolatory letters in his own handwriting, and take into consideration that he was constantly importuned by all kinds of people in his home, fairly overwhelmed with all kinds of questions, and really overburdened with a mass of labor to us almost incredible, we must acknowledge that the sentiment of friendship was with him most remarkably keen and strong, his sympathy deep and lasting. His exhortations were at all times drawn from the innermost sanctuary of faith and love, and distinguished by tenderness and wisdom.

To a woman whose husband had died in consequence of an injury which he had inflicted upon himself, as to the cause of which nothing definite was known, he wrote as follows:*

"Grace and Peace in Christ. Honorable, virtuous Lady. Your son has reported to me the misfortune and misery which have befallen you through the departure of your dear husband, and I am impelled by Christian love to address to you these few words of comfort.

"First of all, let it comfort you, that, in the

---

* Briefe. De Wette, 3, 407.

severe conflict through which your dear husband passed, Christ at length gained the final victory, and that your husband departed in the Lord, in the possession of reason and Christian consciousness. I was beyond measure pleased and delighted to hear this, for thus Christ himself also struggled in the garden, and at length conquered and rose from the dead.

"Although your husband inflicted the fatal injury upon himself, it may be that the devil, who has power over our members, moved his hand by force against his own will; for if he had done it of his own will, he would surely not have come to himself again, nor have made such a confession of faith in Christ. How often does not the devil break people's arms, necks, backs, and all their members! He can exercise his power over the body and members without our will.

"You should, therefore, as I trust you will, bow submissively to God, and count yourself as one of that multitude of whom Christ says (Matt. v. 4): 'Blessed are they that mourn, for they shall be comforted.' All saints must sing the Psalm (xliv. 22): 'For thy sake are we killed all the day long; we are counted as sheep for the slaughter.' There must be sorrow and misfortune, if we are to share the promised comfort.

"Thank God, too, for the great mercy, that your husband was not left in conflict and despair, as some have been, but was by the grace and power of God delivered from these, and found at last steadfast in Christian faith and in God's Word. Of such it is said, Rev. xiv. 13: 'Blessed are they that die in the Lord.' And Christ himself said, John xi. 25: 'Whoso believeth on me, though he were dead, yet shall he live.' With these words may God, the Father, comfort you in Christ Jesus. Amen.

"MARTINUS LUTHER.

"*At Wittenberg, Tuesday Luciæ (Dec. 15), in the year 1528.*"

When M. Johann Cellarius, pastor at Dresden, died in the Lord, April 21, 1541, at the age of forty-six,[*] his widow received from her husband's friend the following letter:[†]

"Grace and Peace in Christ. Honorable, virtuous and dear Lady. I have been pained to learn that God, our dear Father, has suffered his chastening rod to fall upon you, and upon us as well, in taking from you and from us the dear man, M. Johannes Cellarius, your husband, and has thus brought grief upon us all, although we know that

---

[*] Briefe. De Wette, 6, 486.

[†] Ibid., 5, 469.

our friend has entered into sweet, blessed rest. But let it comfort you, that your sorrow is not the greatest among the children of men, many of whom have to suffer and endure that which is a hundred times worse. And though the sufferings of all of us who live upon the earth were gathered upon one heap, they would yet be as nothing compared with that which the Son of God endured for us, and for our salvation; for there is no death worthy to be compared with the death of our Lord and Saviour Jesus Christ, through which we all are saved from eternal death.

"Comfort yourself thus in the Lord, who, though so many times better than we, our husbands, wives, children and all, yet died for you and for us all. We are yet his, whether we die or live, whether in poverty or wealth, or whatever may befall us. If we are his, he is also ours, with all that he has and is. Amen. To his grace I commend you. My Katie wishes you the comfort and favor of God.

"*Monday after Cantate (May 8), 1542.*"

The widow of George Schulze is in few words urged to lay to heart two grounds of consolation.*

"Grace and Peace in the Lord. Honorable, vir-

---

* Briefe. De Wette, 5, 690.

tuous Lady Eva, my good Friend. I am deeply grieved by your misfortune, that God has taken from you your dear husband. I can well believe that such a separation must give you pain. It would not be well if it did not give you pain, for that would be a sign of cold love.

"But, on the other hand, you have, first, the great comfort, that he departed hence in such a Christian and blessed way.

"In the second place, the will of God, our dearest Father, is the very best. He gave his Son for us, and how fitting is it that we should now offer up our wills to the service and pleasure of his will. This we are not only in duty bound to do, but we shall also from the doing of it reap great and eternal fruits of joy. But may he, our dear Lord Jesus Christ, comfort you richly with his Spirit. Amen. I commend you herewith to God.

"*Wednesday after Francisci (Oct. 8), 1544.*"

Very numerous are the letters written by Luther to men whose wives had been called away by death. To his kind and friendly lord and sponsor, Hans of Taubenheim, he writes:*

"Grace and Peace in Christ. Most worthy, steadfast, dear Lord and kind Sponsor. I have

---

*Briefe. De Wette, 5, 141.

learned how our dear Lord God has again suffered his counsel to be wrought out upon you, in taking to himself also your dear wife. This, your sorrow and pain, causes me sincere and heartfelt grief, for I know that your feelings are very different from those of the careless fellows who rejoice in the death of their wives; and I remember, too, that I know you well as one who is surely no enemy of Christ, but who loves his Word and kingdom, and who is thoroughly hostile to all treachery and dishonor, as I have learned by experience. In short, I consider you as a pious man, and in this I am not mistaken; as you also on your part consider me as pious, in which God grant that you may not be mistaken, for I am in greater peril than you, seeing that I am engaged in great affairs, and should therefore (which is the misfortune of my calling) sin the more dangerously if God should withdraw his hand. Since I have this knowledge of you, that you are not an enemy of God, I know also that he on his part cannot be your enemy, having already granted to you not to be his enemy, and having therefore loved you long before you loved him, as has been the case also with us all.

"Bear, then, the stroke of the dear Father's gentle rod in such a way that you may find in his gracious and paternal will towards you a comfort deeper than the pain; and, in the conflict of your grief, let the peace of God, which soars above all our reason and senses, be triumphant, however the flesh may sob and whimper. I am confident that you yourself, taught by the word of God, know without my admonitions that the peace of God must dwell, not in the five senses nor in the reason, but far above in the region of faith. Our dear Lord Jesus Christ be with you. I feel, as God knows, and as I trust you do not doubt, very kindly toward you and cherish earnest love for you. Although I am nothing, and am now of almost no account anywhere, yet Christ must have such a poor, frail, patched-up instrument, and must tolerate me behind the door in his kingdom. May God help me to be worthy of this. Herewith I commend you to God.

"MARTINUS LUTHER.

"*Friday after Day of the Three Kings, in the year 1539.*"

The Magdeburg chancellor, Laurentius Zoch, is thus comforted:*

"May the Grace of God and Peace in Christ be your Comfort, and your Strength. Amen. My dear Doctor and special Friend. I am truly most

---

* Briefe. De Wette, 4, 412. Zoch lived at that time in Halle, but afterwards moved to Wittenberg.

deeply grieved by the great misfortune and sorrow which have fallen upon you, as God has taken from you your dear wife, and, as I learn from your letter, in such a way as must be peculiarly painful.

"Well, so it is. God's Son had not only to be hated and persecuted by the devil and the wicked world, but must at last be called 'smitten of God and humiliated,' as Isaiah liii. 4 says, and the 22d Psalm (verse 6): 'I am a worm and no man.' Thus it must go with us Christians also, that it must be said of us at last in our affliction, that even God himself, from whom we receive all comfort, is punishing us; just as, on the other hand, the ungodly must mount so high that they are regarded as loved and exalted not only by the world, but by God himself, in order that they may doubly mourn in the end.

"Thus has God himself now laid his hand upon you, as it appears, and the enemies can now think and say: 'Thus it goes with Christians. This is the reward which your new Gospel gives you.' This is not only suffering and dying, but also being buried and brought down to hell.

"But, my dear Doctor, only hold fast. Now is the time (for steadfastness). Consider that it went thus and far worse with Christ, and that he, nevertheless, unforsaken of God, whose hand was laid so heavily upon him, came forth with honor. Thus will God lead us also with him.

"It is indeed a great comfort, that your good wife died as a Christian and in the possession of her faculties, and has without doubt gone to Christ, her Lord, whom she here confessed. But it is a much greater comfort, that Christ has formed you in his own likeness, to suffer as he suffered, *i. e.*, to be punished and distressed, not alone by the devil, but as though by God, who is and must be your comfort.

"Therefore, although the flesh indeed murmurs and cries out, as Christ himself also cried out in his weakness (Ps. xxii. 1; Matt. xxvii. 46), yet the spirit should be ready and willing, and with unutterable groaning cry: 'Abba, dear Father' (Rom. viii. 15), that is to say, 'Heavy is thy rod, but I know assuredly that thou art Father still.'

"May our dear Lord and Saviour, who is also our precious example in all suffering, comfort you and impress his own image upon your heart, that you may offer this sacrifice of a mourning spirit, and surrender to him your Isaac. Amen.

"DR. MARTINUS LUTHER.

"*Saturday after All Saints' Day (Nov. 3), in the year 1532.*"

This first epistle he soon followed with another:*

"Grace and Peace in Christ Jesus, our Comfort and our Saviour.—Estimable, learned and dear Lord. I beg you, let me feel assured of your pardon for not sooner answering your letter. Your good friend left too quickly, and I have for several weeks been writing and correcting myself to death, in order not to neglect my beggars and drivers, the printers at Leipzig, so that I was compelled to bind all other letters and lay them aside until I had worked up to time.

"I have read and noted with rejoicing, that God has, partly by means of my former letter, comforted your heart. May the same kind Father carry on to the end the work of comforting which he has begun; for we Christians must become accustomed to that comfort, which is spoken of as 'through patience and comfort of the Scriptures' (Rom. xv. 4).

"Therefore, he often withdraws from us the comfort of visible things, in order that the comfort of the Scriptures may find room and opportunity within us, and not remain standing uselessly in the bare letter without exercise. Thus he has withdrawn from you your excellent comfort and treasure upon earth, in order that he himself may be

* Briefe. De Wette, 4, 419.

your comfort in her place, and compensate you well, although he has already shown to you and others all fidelity, love and comfort.

"We are told that faith consists in that which cannot be seen, and which does not appear (Heb. xi. 1). The ungodly turn their backs upon the wrath of God, which threatens them, but which they do not see, and turn their snouts to that which they can see and feel, and wallow therein like swine. Therefore wrath at last overtakes them suddenly and unexpectedly. But we must turn our faces to the unseen things of grace and to the hidden things of comfort, hoping and waiting upon these; and our backs to things that are seen, that we may accustom ourselves to leave these and depart from them, as St. Paul says: 'Who look not at the things which are seen, but at the things which are unseen (2 Cor. iv. 18).' This gives us pain, as we are unaccustomed to it, and the old Adam draws us back again to the things that are seen, seeking to rest and remain in them. Yet this cannot be, for 'the things which are seen are temporal,' says St. Paul in 2 Cor. iv. 18, and do not endure. Therefore is God called the God of patience and comfort (Rom. xv. 5).

All of this, both such patience and such comfort, is the work of God and beyond our power. This is the school of Christians. They take lessons daily in this art and cannot comprehend it, much less learn it thoroughly, but they always remain children, spelling the A B C of this art.

The rest, that is yet lacking, we must commit to the forgiveness of sins, and offer up through Christ with a paternoster, until that blessed day shall come and make us all perfect in all things. Then shall we be his companions, like Christ, our example, in all things.

"To this may the Father of our Lord Jesus Christ, the God of all comfort, help us all. Amen. Take my prattle kindly.
"DR. MARTIN LUTHER.
"*At Wittenberg, Saturday after Nicolai (December 7), in the year 1532.*"

The squire, Ambrosius Berndt of Jüterbog, who had also lost his wife, received from Luther the following letter of comfort, the beginning and end of which have unfortunately not been preserved.*

"You know, dear Magister, that the mercy of God is greater than our misfortune and our adversity. You have, indeed, as you think, occasion to mourn, but it is nothing but good sugar, mixed with vinegar. A very good thing has happened to your be-

---

* Briefe. De Wette, 6, 190. Berndt was stationed at Wittenberg, 6, 189.

loved wife, for she is now with Christ—she has made a leap. O, would to God that I had also made that leap! I would not greatly long to come back hither again. Do not look only at the vinegar, but take some account also of the sugar. Look upon the misfortunes of other people, that are full of vinegar alone and have no sugar in them.

"Your suffering is only a bodily suffering, namely, the natural love and regard for your family. Your wife died well, and left here nothing better than the memory of a kind, sweet, lovely companionship and obedience. With this you should console yourself, as your heart testifies and proves that you were a kind husband to her and do not forget her. You are a good logician, and a teacher of that art to others; put it into practice now and use right definition, division and conclusion. Learn to divide and separate the spiritual from the carnal. Place your misfortune by the side of that of others, and you will see that the death of your wife is not in itself mournful or pitiful, but only in your inward nature, in which are the natural affections which husband and wife, parents and children, have for one another.

"That was a wise saying of the Emperor Maximilian, and worthy to be held in remembrance, with which he comforted his son, King Philip, who was very deeply grieved and distressed by the death of a faithful, trusty, honorable man who was slain in battle. He said to him: 'Dear Philip, you must get used to it; you will have to lose yet many more who are dear to you.' Thus should honest Christian hearts also do; there is no other way. Satan takes no vacation. He is a liar and murderer, leads people into error and slays them. He practices his wiles even upon Christ, but does not succeed in them. Christ was given over into his hands, but only in order that he might destroy the lord and author of death. Satan is a murderer, but God himself kills no one, for if God should slay, who would go to him? This is not the work nor office of God; but when he withdraws his hand, the devil gobbles us up. God is therefore not efficiently, but privatively, a cause of death; that is, God kills no one, but he permits it to be done and ordains it. It is indeed God's will that we should die, but he has no pleasure in our death.

"Conclusion: God and Satan are most violently opposed to one another. Everything that God does, he does in order that something may be; but Satan labors that it may not be. Satan is therefore an author and source of death, a liar, a murderer. That is his occupation."

Luther often felt himself called upon to write to parents whose sons had been sent in blooming health to the University at Wittenberg, consoling them upon the early death of their dear children in the distant city. We select one of these letters,[*] addressed to a man named Zink, in Königsberg,[†] which no one can read without the deepest emotion:

"First of all, Grace and Peace in Christ our Lord. My dear Friend. I suppose the tidings have already reached you, that your dear son, Johannes Zink, whom you sent to us to pursue his studies here, was taken seriously sick, and that, although there was certainly no lack of attention, care and medicine, yet the disease became too powerful, took him away, and bore him to our Lord Jesus Christ in Heaven.

"He was a very dear boy to us all, especially to me. I have many an evening had him to sing soprano at my house, for he was polite, quiet, modest, and especially diligent in his studies. We are all greatly pained by his departure, and, if it had been at all possible, would most gladly have saved and kept him; but he was much dearer still to God, and he wished to have him.

---

[*] Briefe. De Wette, 4, 362.
[†] Ibid., 6, 638.

"Now it is perfectly natural that this event should grieve and distress your heart and that of your dear wife, as the parents, for which I do not blame you, since it has distressed all of us and especially myself. Yet, I exhort you, give God much rather thanks, that he granted you such a noble and pious child, and counted you worthy to expend your means and labor to such advantage.

"But it ought to afford you, as it does us, the deepest comfort, that he fell asleep, rather than died, so gently and softly, with such admirable confession, faith and reason, that we were all filled with wonder. There can be no doubt—as little as we can doubt the Christian faith itself—that he is blessed forever with God, his true Father. Such a beautiful Christian end cannot fail of the kingdom of heaven.

"You will not forget to consider at the same time, how thankful you should be, and what comfort it should be to you, that he did not perish, as do many others, in peril and misery. And even if he had lived long, you could not, by the outlay of all your means, have helped him to rise higher than perhaps to some position of honor or service; but now he is in the place which he would be utterly unwilling to exchange, even for a moment, for the whole world.

"Though your grief therefore be great, let your comfort be far greater, for you have not lost him, but sent him on before you, that he may be preserved in eternal blessedness. Thus speaks St. Paul (1 Thes. iv. 13): 'Sorrow not over those who are departed, or fallen asleep, as do the heathen, who have no hope.'

"I presume that his preceptor, Magister Veit Dietrich, has reported to you some of his beautiful words spoken before his death, which will gratify and comfort you. But I could not, for love of the good boy, refrain from preparing this letter for you, that you might know by certain proof how it went with him.

"I commend you to our Lord and Comforter, Christ, and to his grace.

"D. M. L.,
"By his own hand, although now also weak.
"*Evening of St. George's Day (April 23), 1532.*"

All who were called to mourn in Wittenberg enjoyed Luther's ministrations of comfort, and if he was prevented from coming to them himself, a letter from his hand was sure to come flying to their home, like a dove with the olive-branch of peace. The only son of the burgomaster, Dr. Benedict Paulus, had a fatal fall while capturing sparrows, when Luther at once wrote to the parents:*

"Although we are nowhere in the Holy Scriptures forbidden to grieve and mourn when a pious child or friend dies, but have, on the other hand, examples of pious patriarchs, forefathers and kings who deeply and sorely bewailed and grieved over the death of their children, yet there must be moderation in such grief and mourning.

"You do no wrong, therefore, dear Doctor, in grieving over the death of your son, if you do not carry it too far, but suffer yourself also to be comforted. Let this then be your comfort: first, that you bear in mind that God gave to you this son and has taken him again; second, that you follow the example of the pious, holy man, Job, who, when he had lost all—children, goods and property, yet said at last (ii. 10 and i. 21): 'Have we received good from the Lord, why will we not also endure evil? The Lord gave, the Lord has taken again. As it pleased the Lord, it has come to pass. Blessed be the name of the Lord.'

"Job rightly considered that both good and evil come from the Lord; and you should do likewise. You will then discover and see that the goods and gifts which God has given and preserved to you

* Briefe. De Wette, 6, 218.

are much more and greater than the evil that you now experience. But you now look only at the evil, namely, that your son has died, and forget meanwhile the great and glorious goods and gifts of God, namely, that he has given you the true knowledge of his Word, that Christ regards you with favor and kindness, and that you have a good conscience, which is alone of itself such a great good, that it should easily outweigh and cover over every evil misfortune that can befall us. No one believes this, unless he has himself experienced and felt what a miserable thing it is to have a conscience filled with terror, which is really and truly death itself and hell. Inasmuch now as you have a good conscience, why are you so distressed and grieved at the death of your son?

"But, granted that the misfortune which has now fallen upon you is a very great and heavy one, yet it is not new, nor has it fallen upon you alone, for you have many companions in this your sorrow and misfortune. Abraham had to experience much greater sorrow of heart for his son, while the latter was yet living, than if he had been dead. For the Lord commanded him to slay him and offer him up with his own hands, although it was his only and well-beloved son, in whose seed God had promised to bless all nations. What do you think must have been the feelings of his heart as he was commanded to behead his son with a naked sword? And do you not think that Jacob must have had great sorrow of heart, when it was reported to him that his dear son, Joseph, had been torn to pieces by wild beasts? Or what father was ever so grieved and distressed as David, when he was so cruelly driven out of his kingdom and persecuted by his son Absalom, whom he had brought up so tenderly? Yea, truly, when Absalom so miserably perished by the spear in that insurrection, and died accursed, the father's heart was no doubt ready to melt.

"Therefore, when you properly remember and consider these and the like examples of high and noble men, you will understand that this your sorrow of heart is not in the least to be compared with theirs, but is much lighter and more endurable.

"But you may say: 'It is my only son that has died.' Why does this so distress and worry you? Just as though God could not give you another, seeing that he is almighty. And even though he should not think good to give another, but should on the other hand take away from you also wife and property, yet you should not on that account grieve and mourn so deeply, since you still have Christ, who regards you with kindness and favor, and you have God as your gracious Father, and, besides all this, many spiritual blessings, which after our death shall remain secure forever.

"'Yes, but he had a horrible and terrible death.' Just as though every death were not horrible, let one die as he may, since death is a terrifying and frightful thing for our human nature, especially to those who have no God. But to us, who are children of God, the terrible image of death becomes endurable, for we have a God who thus comforts us (Jn. xiv. 19): 'As truly as I live, ye shall live also.'

"But you are distressed by the fear that God may have taken your son from you in wrath? Such thoughts do not come from God. But this is the right view:—It was certainly the good and gracious will of God that your son should thus die, however your reason may strive and cry out against it and imagine that God is angry. Reason is always disposed to be well pleased when it can have its own way; but the works of God are at all times totally displeasing to it. It would not therefore be well if our will should be done in every case, for we would then fall into a state of security. Hence, we are satisfied and contented that we have a gracious God. Why he should suffer this or that to come upon us, is a matter with which we should not concern ourselves."

Finally, let us accompany Luther to a house of mourning, that of the painter, Lucas Cranach, to whom we owe the finest and most faithful pictures of Luther. A message has come from Bologna, that John, a promising son of this household, died on the 9th of October, 1536, after witnessing a beautiful and noble Christian confession. The poor parents, in addition to the natural grief of their loving hearts, were enduring also great torment of conscience, as though they themselves were the cause of his death, inasmuch as they had sent him to Italy. On the first day of December, comes Luther, the familiar friend, to the broken-hearted painter, and says:*

"If that were true, I would be as much the cause of his death as you, for I faithfully advised both you and him. But we did not do it with any thought that he should die. Our conscience bears witness that you would much rather know that he was living, yea, that you would much rather die yourself, and lose all your property. Therefore, banish this sting of conscience, for both heart and will, as you should not forget, give very different testimony as to your feelings towards your son." He then turned to the father, who was weeping, and said, "Dear Master Lucas, be calm. God

* Tischreden. Aurif., 325 a. Först., 3, 150.

wishes to break your will. He is apt to lay his hand upon us just where it will give us the most pain, in order to slay our old Adam; and even though our tribulations are not greater than those of other people, yet our own, which we feel, give us the most pain. Think of poor Adam, and what sorrow of heart he had to bear, when his first two sons engaged in fatal strife before his eyes. Think of poor David, who for two whole years bewailed his first-born son, Amnon, slain by his brother Absalom: afterwards, when he learned that Absalom had been slain in his sins and that his body was hanging on a tree, then indeed was there a lamentation; to know that his son was eternally lost, was cause enough for wailing and anguish. In the second place, we should find abundant comfort in the piety and obedience of your dear son, for the world is now so wicked and boorish that even the very noblest youth are led into shame and sin, which might have happened even to him. You see how rough and rude the world is. Sins are openly committed, and boldly denied, so that, even after committing public sins and evil deeds, men dare shamelessly to say: 'My no is worth as much as your yes.'" He then spoke about the rough life of the students, and afterwards told of a certain Magister at Erfurt, who had been a learned and pious man, but, after becoming a priest, became criminally intimate with the wife of a stone-breaker. She was repulsive enough, but he could not keep away from her. Finally, he went to the woman one morning at six o'clock, after he had held mass, and was caught and slain by her husband. "That," said he, "was a terrible death. I have five children, and they are dear to my heart. Yet, when I think of the evil courses of the future, in which they too may become involved, and when I dwell upon the thought, I could wish that they were all dead, for but little improvement is to be expected from the world, as is very evident. In the third place, although it is painful to have lost a pious, obedient son (for one can forget the bad and disobedient more easily than the pious and faithful), yet his obedience and his Christian death should be a joy to you, for the hour of his departure was a good and blessed one, chosen for him by God. O blessed and thrice blessed is he, who passes safely through that hour! It is my daily longing and petition, that God may grant me a happy, blessed parting-hour, for then shall I know that it has been good for me to be here, and that, released from all misery and affliction, I shall be happy with God. In the fourth place, dear Master Lucas, commit this matter to God, the most high Father, who has more interest in your son than you. You are only his father according to the flesh, and have only for a little while trained and nourished him; but God gave to him his body and soul, has ever guarded and kept him, and is much, much more a father to him than you. He must and can keep, care for and nourish him better than you or the whole world. In the fifth place, let there be a limit to your grief and mourning. Forget it altogether. Commit it to the will of God, which is better than ours. Not evil, but good, has befallen your son. Eat and drink, refresh yourself, and do not thus worry yourself to death, for you have yet work to do for other people. Sadness and distress dry up the bones."

CHAPTER VI.

HOW LUTHER STRENGTHENED THE TEMPTED.

LUTHER felt the deepest compassion for all who were tempted, for he had himself passed through temptations the most severe, galling to the flesh, and bringing down the soul to the gates of hell, so that he could truthfully say of himself that he was scarcely able to gasp or draw his breath, and that he went about parched and withered like a shadow.* He had himself, as he was accustomed to express it, lain in this hospital,† and had, by the great grace of God, entirely recovered. He, if any one, must understand how to deal with the tempted, to strengthen and, by the help of God, heal them. "I have learned by experience," he says,‡ "how one should act under temptation, namely, when any one is afflicted with sadness, despair or other heart-sorrow, or has a worm gnawing in his conscience, let him first lay

---

* Tischreden. Aurif., 315 a. Först., 3, 121.

† Briefe. De Wette, 4, 247. Tischreden. Aurif., 314, b. Först., 3, 119.

‡ Tischreden. Aurif., 319 a. Först., 3, 132.

hold of the comfort of the divine Word, and then let him eat and drink and seek the companionship and conversation of pious Christian people, and he will soon be better."

His view as to the proper course to be pursued by the tempted is very fully expressed in a commentary upon Isaiah xxxvi. 11, as follows:*

"This is an excellent passage, which contains a doctrine great and precious beyond measure, showing how we should conduct ourselves in great temptations. When Eliakim and Shebna propose and undertake to quiet Rabshakeh a little and make him milder by humbling themselves before him, they fail utterly; for they thereby only make him more insolent and bold, and whet the devil's tongue. King Hezekiah therefore afterwards advises them to make no reply whatever to the blasphemy of the enemy.

"Thus should we also do in our temptations, whether they assail the body or beset the spirit and the conscience. Although human reason can not be content until it has looked about for human help, as did also the servants of King Hezekiah, yet we should accustom ourselves, and put ourselves most carefully on guard, not to answer the devil when we fall into temptation, nor dispute

* Werke. Walch, 6, 689 ff.

with him, nor allow ourselves to be drawn into much talking. For I can testify from experience, that the more you give way to the thoughts with which the devil attacks and wearies you, the more vigorously and quickly does he set himself against you, until at length he drives you to despair.

"Look, for example, at the trifling temptation to impurity, which assails chiefly the young. The more an impure disposition and heart thinks about love and lust, the more it is inflamed. It occurs sometimes that a little spark, when a strong wind happens to strike it, becomes a great fire; and thus love, let it be trifling and weak as it may, when indulged, becomes strong. It is the same also with hatred and envy; for if a man is constantly considering how he will avenge himself, he will soon be driven by such thoughts to some reckless deed.

"Therefore, just as in these bodily temptations there is only one solitary way to overcome, namely, to turn away from them the senses, the thoughts, and the heart; so also in spiritual temptations there is no other counsel, and no better help, nor more powerful remedy, than that one cast such thoughts out of his mind more and more, as best he can, and think upon the very opposite.

"Although this is far beyond the ability of man, yet certain ways and methods may be suggested, by which such thoughts, if not entirely overcome and utterly banished, may yet be reduced to the smallest dimensions. Therefore, whenever any one is assailed by temptation of any sort whatever, the very best that he can do in the case is either to read something in the Holy Scriptures, or to think about the Word of God, and take it in hand and to his heart. And even though there should be no desire in the heart to read or to consider the Word of God (for the devil takes wonderful delight in hindering it and awakening aversion to it), still you should compel yourself to do this, so that, even if your heart and thoughts will not lay hold of it, your tongue and ears and eyes may yet be employed upon it, and may thus be led to see, hear and do other things than what the mind and heart think about and purpose. You will certainly find that, if the outward senses are occupied with the Word, the mind and heart will also easily be led to it. Just here is especially seen the power and might of the Word of God, namely, that, in the most admirable way, it heals and restores again to health the mind and heart of man when wounded by the arrows of the devil.

"Therefore Isaiah, in the ninth chapter of his

prophecy (verse 6), among other names of Christ, has mentioned also this, that he is a Counselor of the afflicted and the tempted; for Christ comforts people by means of his precious Word, as he also declares in the 50th chapter of Isaiah (verse 4): 'The Lord hath given me a learned tongue, that I should know how to speak a word in season to the weary.' St. Paul also teaches likewise, in Romans xv. 14, that we should obtain and strengthen hope from the comfort of the Holy Scriptures, which the devil endeavors to tear out of people's hearts in times of temptation. Accordingly, as there is no better nor more powerful remedy in temptations than to cast the disturbing thoughts out of the mind and heart, so there is for this purpose no other but this one single way, namely, to diligently read and hear the Word of God. Thus can we best of all quench the fiery darts of the devil. But those who will not follow this advice, but cling to the grievous and disturbing thoughts, only keep on laying more wood and straw upon the fire, until they are worn out, and, overcome by the devil, who has a thousand arts to practice, give up in despair. This one line of attack the devil pursues to the utmost against us, undertaking to break down our faith and confidence by the thought that God is angry with us. If you now attempt, in this spiritual conflict, to protect yourself by the help of man without the Word of God, you simply enter upon the conflict with that mighty spirit, the devil, naked and unprotected. You may, therefore, if you so please, oppose your power to the might of the devil. It will then be very easily seen what an utterly unequal conflict it is, if one do not have at hand in the beginning the Word of God (which, as St. Paul writes in Rom. i. 16, is alone the power of God), for any one without the Word of God to strive and contend by human power and human means against the devil, who has from the beginning of the world come off conqueror on so many a field, and who is such a practiced and experienced warrior.

"Therefore, pay no attention to the thoughts with which the devil seeks to occupy your heart, and by all means be on your guard, lest you be drawn into dispute with him. He can transform himself into an angel of light, and can assume the likeness of the glorious person of Christ. Since he is also acquainted with the Holy Scriptures, as may be seen in the fourth chapter of Matthew, he employs at times even the most precious words of Christ himself against Christ and against the faith. If now, in such temptations, you do not at once turn away your heart and mind, and say: 'I know nothing of any other Christ than he whom the Father gave and who died for me and for my sins, and I know that he is not angry with me, but is kind and gracious to me; for he would not otherwise have had the heart to die for me and for my benefit' — if one do not hold up this and the like before the devil, and cast himself with diligence upon the Holy Scriptures to read them faithfully, he will be compelled to give up in despair; for the devil can very easily quench the weak little spark of our faith, if we do not constantly increase, strengthen and improve it by the Word of God.

"Further, that which we now mention is a trifling, but yet a necessary and useful measure, namely, that when any one is sad and melancholy he should not be alone, but should make an effort to fall into conversation, no matter upon what subject, with some good friends; for when one talks with another, the heart is drawn from grievous thoughts. Lonely places are therefore in times of temptation beyond measure injurious and dangerous. Hence King Solomon says rightly in Eccl. iv. 10: 'Woe unto him who is alone; for if he fall, he hath not another to help him up.' The word of a fellow-christian has wonderful power. Therefore all those who are entangled in temptations should know and remember that the voice and words of their brethren and fellow-christians are to be heard and believed as the word and voice of God himself, as though God himself were speaking to them. And if one could find no such preacher, nor any person who could comfort with the Word of God, it would yet be better to listen to the conversation of other people, than to let the devil speak his blasphemies and shoot his fiery arrows into our hearts.

"I have, in these general precepts, rules and doctrines, proposed and indicated the proper course to be pursued in times of temptation. It now remains for every one to so direct his mind and heart in this matter against the devil, that he may discover that this my well-meant counsel and opinion has not been without benefit to him. Let no one who has committed himself to the Christian faith for a moment cherish the thought that he can live without temptation; for the saying of St. Paul to Timothy (second epistle iii. 12) is true, that 'All who would live godly in Christ Jesus shall suffer persecution.'

"Now bodily temptations, such as poverty, avarice, boastfulness, shame, and the like, can be easily overcome. But it requires effort and labor, when the devil holds up before us the wrath of God, and when, in addition, our own conscience comes to his assistance with its testimony and convicts us, being itself burdened and highly wrought up by the devil, who points out many examples of the wrath of God presented in the Holy Scriptures and daily occurring. This, then, is the most furious and sudden of all attacks, in which the devil exerts to the full extent all his powers and arts, and transforms himself into the likeness of the angry and ungracious God. If you now begin to indulge the thoughts which the devil suggests and insinuates, you are already lost and ruined. But many people do this, and we see, in consequence, how they tumble about and fall. They would like to escape from the grievous and startling thoughts of the wrath of God, and hence they hang, stab or drown themselves, or in some other way destroy and kill themselves. When the devil has brought this to pass, he has accomplished his designs; for, when he has once turned our eyes away from Christ, he at once sets himself to work to drive us also to despair.

"One should therefore banish from his mind and heart the grievous thoughts of sin and of the wrath of God, and cherish the very opposite thoughts; as we read in the 'Lives of the Ancient Fathers' of a certain one, who, being at one time beset with great temptations to despair on account of a sin which he had committed, finally aroused himself and said: 'Why, I have committed no sin; I did not do it.'

Not that he disowned or denied the sin, but he found that he could in no other way escape from the grievous thoughts than by casting them out of his mind and cherishing the opposite thoughts. It was, especially if he spoke these words from confidence in the death and merits of Christ, a great example of a noble faith, which we would do well to follow when in similar peril and temptation. We should also learn from it, that we should not dispute with the devil; otherwise, the weak and timid will be so overwhelmed by grievous thoughts, that they may take their own lives; for the spirit and heart of man is not able to endure the thought of the wrath of God, as the devil represents and urges it. Therefore, whatever thoughts the devil awakens within us in temptation we should put away from us and cast out of our minds, and close our ears and eyes against them, so that we may see and hear nothing else than the kind, comforting word of the promise of Christ, and of the gracious will of the Heavenly Father, who has given his own Son for us, as Christ, our dear Lord, declares in John iii. 16: 'God so loved the world that he gave his only begotten Son, that whosoever believeth on him should not perish, but have everlasting life.' Everything else, now, which the devil may suggest to us beyond this, that God the Father is reconciled to us, and graciously inclined to us, and merciful for the sake of his dear Son, we should cast out of our minds as wandering and unprofitable thoughts.

"Instruction similar to this is given by Gerson, the pious, honest Doctor, who alone of all the latest theologians has anything upon this subject, and who exerted himself faithfully to comfort timid consciences; the others all seem to have spent their days in rioting and good living, and never devoted a single word to this lofty doctrine and the consolation which so many need. Gerson gives a very appropriate illustration, comparing these thoughts of the devil, with which he pierces the hearts of Christians as with fiery darts, to a barking dog. If you throw anything at a barking dog, or strike at him, it only makes him worse; and just so is it, says Gerson, with evil thoughts in temptations. As it is the best way to pay no attention to the barking of the dog, but pass quietly by, so it is the only wise plan in temptations to despise and cast out the thoughts and suggestions of the devil, and not suffer one's self to be drawn into further disputation or quarrel with him; the evil thoughts will then disappear of themselves. The more one worries himself and quarrels with them, the more they press upon him and harass him. It is impossible by human reason or power to overcome and cast out the grievous, poisonous thoughts of the devil; but there is nothing so hard for him to endure as that he should be despised. They, therefore, do the very best thing, who are able to remain firm and strong in such temptations, and despise the wicked enemy, the devil.

"Very similarly, we read also in the 'Lives of the Ancient Fathers' of a certain one, who asked his brother to advise him what to do, as grievous thoughts often came suddenly into his mind. The latter thereupon advised him that, as these thoughts came of themselves, so he should let them go of themselves again, and only not give himself up to them. 'For just,' said he, 'as it is not in your power to forbid the birds to fly in the air over your head, although you can prevent them from making their nests in your hair; so, too, you cannot protect yourself from the thoughts of the devil, but give all diligence that the thoughts of the devil do not take and hold entire possession of your heart, mind and spirit, for, if it comes to that, you are lost.' This ancient father taught rightly and gave good advice. If we do not wish to place ourselves in peril, we must follow the same course; for the more we give way to these thoughts, the less able shall we be to get rid of them, and, as though locked up in an intricate building or labyrinth, we shall never become free and escape from them.

"We have an example of this in the case before us. They attempt to satisfy Rabshakeh by courtesy and good counsel; but it is all in vain. He only becomes more violent and bold. I desire therefore most faithfully to commend to you this history, that you may know what counsel and help should be given to tempted and timid consciences. I have known many such, who, when very great and sudden temptations have assailed them, did not understand the art of despising and casting out these thoughts, and in consequence lost their minds and became violently insane; and some, when their minds had become too severely strained by these startling thoughts, took their own lives.

"Now such thoughts are nothing but a web spun by the devil, which we do not make or do, but suffer; they are not the works of men, but their sufferings. For those who will not learn this, all is lost; for they must go to destruction. The devil is such a proud spirit, that he is never weary until he vanquishes and wins the day. Before those who do not despise him, but give attention to him, he displays one scene after another, hurling upon them one thought after another, until they are overpowered and destroyed. Those now who desire to escape the wiles of the devil, should say to him: I will be neither spectator nor fiddler for you; for Christ himself has reminded us, Matt. xviii. 3: 'Except ye be converted and become as little children, ye shall not enter into the kingdom of heaven.' Thus, as long as the servants of King Hezekiah dispute with Rabshakeh and notice him, he becomes only bolder and more violent. But King Hezekiah rebukes them, as the narrative further tells us, and says to them: 'Why do you answer him?'"

In connection with this fundamental passage, in which the Reformer expresses most fully and in systematic order his views as to the proper treatment of the tempted, we present also a few of his utterances bearing upon separate phases of the subject.

Luther was accustomed to discriminate between the different forms of temptation. He declares expressly:* "But there are two kinds of temptation, namely, of the spirit and of the body. Satan vexes and alarms the conscience with lies, reviling and perverting even that which has been rightly and well done, and in accordance with the Word of God; he vexes the body in other ways." No attempt is here made accurately to define spiritual

---

*Tischreden. Aurif., 310, a.   Först., 3, 105.

temptation, for he well knows that there are many kinds of spiritual temptation, and he here presents only the worst form.

"The temptation of faith," he says again,* "is the very greatest and most severe, for it is the province of faith to overcome all other temptations. If now faith itself be vanquished, we are at the mercy of all other temptations, even the very smallest and weakest. But, if faith remains undisturbed, we can despise the very greatest temptations and dangers; for if faith be sound and healthy, all other temptations must grow weaker and disappear. This temptation of faith was St. Paul's thorn in the flesh, a great roasting-fork or pole driven through spirit and flesh, through body and soul. It was not a temptation of incitement to fleshly lust, as the Papists dream because they themselves have never felt any other. The great conflicts they have never engaged in, and know nothing of them from their own experience; hence they speak and write of them as the blind speak of color." By the temptation of faith is meant that the evil conscience drives out of a person his confidence in the pardoning grace of God, and leads him to imagine that God is angry and wishes the death of the sinner; or that, in other words, the conscience

---

* Tischreden. Aurif., 316 b. Först. 3, 125.

places Moses upon the judgment-seat, and casts down the Saviour of sinners from the throne of grace. "This is the strongest, greatest and severest temptation of the devil, that he says: 'God is an enemy of sinners; you are a sinner, therefore God is your enemy.'"* Again and again he comes back to the declaration, that this is the noose which Satan throws over the head of the poor child of man in order to strangle him.† "This temptation," he remarks,‡ "is felt more by one person than by another, and in different form. To me, Satan casts up my evil deeds and words, as, that I held mass and thus blasphemed God, or that I did this or that in my youthful days: others, again, he vexes by casting up to them the wicked life which they have led."

He who is tempted should comfort himself with the reflection, that temptation is the very thing which the Christian is called upon to suffer. "Let every one," says Luther,‖ "who wishes to be a genuine Christian remember that without temptation he cannot learn Christ." At another time he says:§ "The God-fearing man is chastened in

* Tischreden. Aurif., 303 b. Först., 3, 78.
† Ibid., 317 a, 327 b. Först., 3, 126, 160, 159.
‡ Ibid., 303 b. Först., 3, 78.
‖ Ibid., 303 b. Först., 3, 79.
§ Ibid., 313 b. Först., 3, 116.

order that he may not be condemned with the world; but the ungodly, in order that he may either learn to know himself or become the more hardened. The better the Christian, the more temptation; the greater the sin, the more fear."

The tempted man has also the consolation of knowing that he is not the only one who is thus vexed. "Be of good cheer," he once exclaimed to Dr. Jerome Weller, as they were sitting at table,* "you are not the only one who is assailed by temptation; I am another, and I have much greater sins to account for than you and your fathers. I would rather that I had been a whoremonger and robber than to have sacrificed and blasphemed Christ in the mass for fifteen years."

Further, the temptations of the Christian are good for him. "But such temptations," says he consolingly,† "are not only necessary, but also good and useful; without them, we would go on in security, with no fear of God before our eyes and never calling upon him for help, for he who is well and happy has no need of physician or comforter. Thus the devil might easily deceive us. Temptation, however, teaches us to live in the fear of God, to pray without ceasing, to grow in the grace and

---

*Tischreden. Aurif., 315 a. Först., 3, 119.
†Ibid., 309 b. Först., 3, 104.

knowledge of Christ, and to understand the power of the Word; and, although we still remain weak, yet the power of our Lord Christ is mighty in the weak."

Hence, temptations are not indications of wrath, but just the opposite, *i. e.*, indications of the paternal love of God. As the excellent pastor, Johann Schlaginhaufen of Köthen, who was strongly inclined to melancholy, was upon one occasion dining with Luther, the Reformer said:* "It is impossible that the heart of man should learn to know God aright and hold him in remembrance and think of him, without enduring temptation and the dear cross." Then, turning to his sorrowful friend, he added: "Believe me, if you did not stand so high in the favor of God, you would not have to endure such trial and temptation." "Let it be granted," said he at another time,† "that God appears to be angry when we are vexed and tempted; yet, if we repent and believe, we shall come to see that beneath the wrath of God lie hidden grace and goodness, just as his strength and power lie concealed beneath our weakness. So long as we remain steadfast in hope and wait patiently, we do not allow such masks to offend or disturb us, but pray diligently."

*Tischreden. Aurif., 315 a. Först., 3, 120.
† Ibid., 318 b. Först., 3, 131.

He who is assailed by temptation should bury himself in the Holy Scriptures. He should diligently hear and read them, should meditate deeply upon them and lay them to heart. But especially does Luther direct such to the Gospel, as foretold by by the prophets, and presented in fulfilment in the New Testament. Not the entire Scriptures, but only those portions which set forth the Lord Jesus Christ, quicken and lift up. The law can only accuse and condemn. "Is any one," says he,* "in temptation, or in the company of those who are tempted, let him smite Moses to death, and cover him all up with stones. But when the tempted one is restored again to health and delivered from the temptation, then preach the law to him; for when one is distressed we should not add to his anxiety."

On another occasion, he sets forth this comfort of the Gospel as follows:† "It is a falsehood, that God is an enemy of sinners, for Christ roundly and plainly declares, by commandment of the Father: 'I am come to save sinners.' But if the devil holds up before you Sodom and other examples of the divine wrath, hold up before him Christ, who became man and for our sakes crept into our poor

---

*Tischreden. Aurif., 314 a. Comp. 305 a. Först., 3, 117 and 83.

†Ibid., 303 b. Först., 3, 79.

flesh and blood, yet without sin. Now if God were an enemy of sinners, he certainly would not have given his only-begotten Son for them. We should learn to understand this thoroughly, for it is good and useful for us, and not, as some imagine, a vain and empty thing."

Luther was accustomed to warn the tempted against spending much of their time alone. Thus he urged upon Dr. Weller, that he in his "sorrow, temptation and distress should seek company and by no means be alone, nor creep off by himself to torment and torture himself with his own thoughts and the suggestions of the devil, for the Holy Spirit says (Eccl. iv. 10): 'Woe to him who is alone.' When I am dispirited and melancholy, I flee from loneliness, go among the people and talk with them. Christ himself was tempted of the devil in the lonely wilderness, but the wilderness was not lonely for John the Baptist, as there were people living round about."* "This, my dear Doctor," he proceeds,† "is the one chief thing; see to it that you do not stay alone when you are tempted. Yes, flee from loneliness, as did the monk, who said when assailed by temptation in his cell: 'I will not stay here; I will leave my cell

---

* Tischreden, 317 a. Först., 3, 127.
† Ibid., 317 b. Först., 3, 127.

and go to my brethren.'" He was fond of quoting a striking saying of Cardinal Albrecht of Mentz, that the human heart is like a mill-stone. As long as grain is fed to the latter, it goes round, grinds, crushes, and turns out meal. But when the supply of grain fails, the mill-stone goes round all the same, but now grinds itself, and becomes thinner and smaller. Thus also the human heart must have something to do. If it does not have the works of its calling to occupy it, the devil comes and casts in temptation, despondency and sadness. Then the heart wears itself away with sadness, until it almost perishes from weakness, and many a one worries himself to death, as Sirach says (xxx. 25): "Sadness kills many people," devouring the bones and marrow, and is of no benefit whatever.*

Instead of giving himself up in loneliness to his own thoughts, and thus sinking ever deeper in the mire, let the tempted one go out to his field of labor, address himself to the works of his calling, and do his duty. "As Dr. Martin Luther was upon one occasion† leaving the castle-church after preaching there, he was met by a common soldier, very poorly clad, who complained that he was

---

* Tischreden. Aurif., 317 b. Först., 3, 128.

† Ibid., 494, b. Först., 4, 255.

sorely tempted by the devil, whom he seemed actually to see and hear, and who was constantly trying to take him away. As they were thus conversing, Dr. Pommer also approached, and they both sought to comfort the poor soldier, urging him not to yield to despair, for although he was tempted by the devil, yet he did not belong to him, and reminding him that the Lord Christ was also tempted of the devil and led into the wilderness, afterwards also to a pinnacle of the temple and upon an exceeding high mountain, and that nevertheless the Lord Christ had overcome him with the Word of God and prayer. Then said Dr. Martin Luther further: 'If the devil vexes you and threatens to take you away, say to him: I belong to the Lord Christ, in whom I believe, and who has promised that he will himself take me away and that no one shall snatch his Christians out of his hand. Again, the Lord Christ himself says (John xvii. 12): "Father, of those whom thou hast given me have I lost none!" You ought to believe in God far too strongly to be so much afraid of the devil and his cunning, for although he would indeed gladly take you away, yet he is not able to do it. A thief would like very much to steal a rich man's money and treasures out of his chest, but he cannot do it. Thus God does not allow the devil to have his own way so far as to bring any real injury or sorrow upon you. Only listen to God's Word, pray diligently, believe, work faithfully, and do not stay alone often, and God will surely deliver you from the devil and preserve you.'"

At another place we are told* of "a young apprentice in the employ of a locksmith," who "was led up and down through all the streets of the city by a ghost. He was examined one morning from six until nine o'clock by Dr. Martin Luther, in the presence of other learned men and trustworthy people, and was asked whether he had learned the catechism. But he declared, under the prompting of the evil spirit, that he had sinned against God in receiving the sacrament in both elements, and reported that the devil had finally said to him: 'If you go into your master's house, I will break your neck.' He had therefore not entered it for several days. Then said Dr. Martin Luther: 'We must not believe every one just at once, for many persons often imagine such things; and even if he did see the ghost, he ought not to have forsaken his calling.' He then questioned him further, and asked him what he had said to Satan, saying: 'See that you tell the truth now. Fear God, hear his Word with dili-

*Tischreden. Aurif., 306 a. Först., 3, 87.

gence, go to your master's house and work at your calling, and if the devil comes again, say to him: I won't listen to you, but to my God who has called me to this position and trade. I will follow my calling, even though an angel from heaven should come and tell me not to do so.'"

That many persons are assailed by temptations because they do not give due attention to the body, but treat it improperly, the Reformer knew very well, and he therefore urges the tempted to eat and drink. He was fond of relating "the history of a certain bishop, whose sister, living in a convent, was sorely distressed by a spirit of sadness and by evil dreams, and temptations, and utterly refused to be comforted. She made a visit to her brother and told him of her trouble. The brother ordered a splendid supper, invited his sister as a guest, and urged her to eat and drink heartily, which she did. The next morning the bishop asked her how she had slept, and whether she had been troubled with dreams and temptations during the night. 'No,' said she, 'I slept very well and had no temptation.' Then said the bishop: 'My dear sister, go home again and take good care of your body, eating and drinking to spite the devil, and you will find that evil dreams and temptations will no longer trouble you.' Therefore, said Dr. Martin, we ought to refresh sorrowful persons with food and drink. But this means alone may not answer, especially for young people."*

The letters of Luther reveal to us how deeply he was moved to compassion for all those who were assailed by temptation, and how he sought in brotherly love to strengthen them from his own rich experience. Hearing that the Captain of Nordhausen, Jonas of Stockhausen, has grown weary of life, the Reformer hastens to his help.†

"Grace and Peace in Christ. Your Worship, my dear and firm Friend. It is reported to me by good friends that the wicked enemy is sorely assailing you with disgust of life and desire for death. O, my dear Friend, now it is high time that you should give up trusting your own thoughts and following them, and listen to other people, who have escaped from the power of this temptation. Press your ear close to our lips, and let our word go straight down into your heart, and God will comfort and strengthen you through our word.

"In the first place, you know that we ought to and must be obedient to God, and guard ourselves diligently against disobedience to his will. Since now you cannot but understand, and be very sure,

---

* Tischreden. Aurif., 319 a. Först., 3, 133.
† Briefe. De Wette, 4, 415.

that God gives you life and does not yet wish to see you die, your thoughts should certainly yield to this divine will, and you should be willingly obedient to God and have no doubt that such thoughts, being contrary to the will of God, are most certainly hurled and driven by force into your heart by the devil. You must therefore set yourself firmly against them, and, in turn, by force bear up against them or cast them out.

"Life was very bitter for our Lord Christ also, but he would not die without his Father's will, fled from death and preserved his life as long as he could, saying: 'Mine hour is not yet come.' So also Elijah and Jonah, and other prophets, in great misery and out of patience with life, called and cried for death, cursing their very birth, their day and their life; yet they had to live and bear the burden with all their power or weakness until their appointed hour had come.

"To such words and examples, as the words and admonitions of the Holy Spirit, you must give honest heed, rejecting and casting out the thoughts that lead you to oppose them. If you find it a hard and bitter task to do this, just think of yourself as a prisoner bound in chains, from which you must struggle and worry to free yourself, until the sweat rolls from your body. The devil's arrows, when they are so deeply imbedded, cannot be drawn out by laughter nor without labor, but must be torn out by force.

"Therefore you must pluck up courage and confidence against yourself, and, angry with yourself, exclaim: 'No, my friend, if you were twice as unwilling to live, yet you must and shall live, for my God desires, and I desire, to have it so. Away with you, thoughts of the devil! Get you to the abyss of hell with dying and death. Here there is nothing for you to do,' etc. Set your teeth together against these thoughts, and, relying on God's will, lift up your head firmly, and make yourself more stiff-necked and stubborn than the rudest peasant, yes, harder than any iron anvil.

"If you lay hold of yourself in this way and fight against yourself, God will assuredly help you. But if you will not thus shut yourself up and protect yourself, but allow your thoughts to vex you as they please in every moment of leisure, you will soon lose the day.

"But the very best advice of all is, not to be all the time trying to contend with these thoughts, but to despise them if you can. Act as if you did not notice them, but were always thinking about something else, and say to them: 'All right, Devil, but let me alone now; I can't attend to your thoughts just now, for I must take a ride or a drive, or eat or drink, or do this or that'; or, 'I must be cheerful now, come again to-morrow,' etc.; or, do anything else that you can think of, play or make sport if you please, only so that you thoroughly and truly despise such thoughts, and drive them away from you, though it be with rude, coarse words, such as: 'Dear Devil, can't you come a little closer to me; I am pining to have you near!' For examples of this, get some one to read to you about the Skin-flint and about the Goose-piper, etc., in Gerson's 'Upon Blasphemous Thoughts.' This is the best counsel that can be given. Our prayers and those of all pious Christians will help you to follow it.

"I herewith commend you to our dear Lord, the only Saviour and true Conqueror, Jesus Christ. May he gain his victory and celebrate his triumph over the devil in your heart, and give us all cause for rejoicing in the help granted you and the wonders wrought in you; which we confidently hope and pray, as he has bidden and commanded us. Amen.

"Dr. Martinus Luther.

"*At Wittenberg. Wednesday after Katharinæ (Nov. 27, 1532).*"

The faithful friend and spiritual adviser does not

fail to give special advice to the wife of the tempted man. Under the same date, he writes to her:*

"Grace and Peace in Christ. Honorable, virtuous Lady. I have hastily written a short letter of encouragement to your dear husband. Now the devil is an enemy to both of you, because you love his enemy Christ. For that you must be made to suffer, as Christ himself says (John xv. 19): 'Because I have chosen you, therefore the world and the prince of the world hate you, but be of good cheer.' The suffering of his saints is precious in the sight of God.

"I can write but little now, as I am greatly hurried. But let me urge you not to leave your husband alone for a single moment, nor to leave anything within his reach with which he might harm himself. Solitude is a real poison for him, and the devil therefore tries to keep him alone. If some one would read a great deal to him out of histories, talk and read about recent happenings and strange things, it would do no harm, even if they were sometimes foolish trifles and false tales of Turks, Tartars and the like, in order to arouse him, if possible, to laugh and joke; then let the advantage be quickly followed up with comforting texts of

* Briefe. De Wette, 4, 417.

Scripture. But whatever you do, do not let him be alone, nor in any place where all is quiet about him, so that he can give himself up to his own thoughts. No matter if he gets angry with you for disturbing him. Act as though you were offended, and scold him; but be all the more careful to carry out your plan. I trust you will accept these lines written in haste. Christ, who has brought this heart-sorrow upon you, will help you, as he has lately helped you in your own trouble. But only stand firm. You are the apple of his eye; who touches it, touches him. Amen."

In the days of Luther, many minds were occupied and disturbed by the question of the divine fore-ordination or predestination. We have already seen, in the example of Albrecht of Mansfeld, how this question in many instances led to reckless levity; but in very many cases it produced great anxiety and melancholy. The pious Barbara Lisskirchen (often shortened to Lischner) was such a tormented soul. Luther seeks to strengthen her by the complete discussion of the subject in the following letter:*

"Grace and Peace in Christ. Virtuous' and dear Lady. Your dear brother, Jerome Weller, has informed me that you are deeply distressed by

* Briefe. De Wette, 4, 247.

temptation upon the subject of eternal predestination. I am truly sorry to hear this. Amen. May Christ, our Lord, deliver you from this temptation. Amen.

"I know all about this sickness; I was myself brought down to the verge of eternal death in this hospital. Now, besides my prayer for you, I would gladly counsel and comfort you, but it is a hard thing to discuss such matters in writing; yet I will try to do it as well as I can, if God will grant me the needed grace. I will tell you how God helped me out of the trouble, and by what means I even yet daily guard myself against it.

"In the first place, you must firmly fix it in your heart, that such thoughts are most certainly the suggestions and fiery darts of the miserable devil. Thus the Scriptures declare, as is said in Prov. xxv. 27: 'He who searches out the lofty affairs of Majesty shall be crushed.' Now such thoughts are nothing but a searching out of the divine Majesty, an attempt to search out God's lofty predestination. Jesus, the son of Sirach, says (iii. 22): 'Thou shalt not search out that which is too high for thee, but concern thyself with that which God has commanded thee; for it will profit thee nothing to be gaping after that which is not commanded thee.' And David also sadly acknowledges, Ps. cxxxi. 1, that he has fared badly when he has attempted to search out high things.

"Therefore it is certain that this comes not from God, but from the devil. He vexes the heart with it, in order that men may become alienated from God and give way to despair, which God has yet strictly forbidden in the first commandment, in which he calls upon us to love, and praise Him in whom we live.

"In the second place, when such thoughts come to you, you should learn to say: 'My dear, in which commandment is it written that I must think or bother myself about that?' If no commandment can be found, then learn to say: 'Ah! away with you, you miserable Devil, you want to compel me to care for myself, when God everywhere says that I shall let him care for me, declaring: "I am thy God," that is, "I care for you; depend upon me, observe what I command you, and let me have the care, as St. Peter teaches (I. v. 7): 'Cast all your care upon him, for he careth for you,' and David (Ps. lv. 22): 'Cast thy burden upon the Lord, and he shall sustain thee.'"

"In the third place, although the thoughts do not now give up troubling you (for the devil is always slow to give up), yet you, on your part, must also refuse to give up, and still turn your heart away from them, and say: 'Do you not hear, Devil? I will have nothing to do with such thoughts. God, too, has forbidden them. Away with you! I must now think of his commandments and in the meanwhile let him take care of me. If you are so wise in such matters, go up to Heaven and dispute with God himself; he can answer you fully enough.' Thus you must always put him off and turn your heart to God's commandments.

"In the fourth place, the very highest among all the commandments of God is this, that we ever hold up before us his dear Son, our Lord Jesus Christ. He must daily be to our hearts the perfect mirror, in which we see how God loves us, and how he, as a faithful God, has so grandly cared for us as to give his own dear Son for us.

"Here, here, I say, and nowhere else, do we learn the right way to deal with this question of predestination. This will prove that you believe on Christ. If you believe, then you are called; if you are called, then you are most certainly also predestinated. Let not this mirror and throne of grace be torn away from before your eyes, but when such thoughts come and sting like fiery serpents, do not look at the thoughts and serpents, but turn your eyes at once away and look upon the brazen serpent, that is, Christ given for us, and, if it please

God, you will soon feel better. But it takes, as I have said, a struggle, and a constant driving away of the evil thoughts. If they drop into your mind, let them drop out again, just as any one would quickly spit out dung, if it should fall into his mouth.

"Thus God has helped me. It is his earnest commandment that we keep before us the image of his Son, who has abundantly proved himself to be our God, as the first commandment teaches, and who promises that he will help and care for us. Therefore he will not suffer us to help or care for ourselves. That would be to deny God, and at the same time, the first commandment and Christ as well.

"The miserable devil, who is an enemy of God and Christ, tries by such thoughts, in direct opposition to the first commandment, to tear us away from Christ and God and lead us to think about ourselves and our own cares, so that we may assume the office of God, which is to care for us and be our God; just as he in Paradise sought to make Adam a god, so that Adam might be his own god, and care for himself, and rob God of this divine work of caring for him,—in which attempt Adam so horribly fell.

"This much I have wanted to say to you for this time, and I have written to your brother, Jerome Weller, that he too should diligently warn and exhort you to let such thoughts alone and to send the devil back to his home to sound all their depths. He knows very well how it went with him when he thus meddled with things too high for him, that he fell from Heaven into the abyss of hell.

"The conclusion of the whole matter is, that what is not commanded should not be allowed to lead us astray nor disturb us. It comes from the instigation of the devil and not from God. May our dear Lord Jesus Christ show you his hands and feet, and speak kindly greeting to your heart, that you may look upon and listen to him alone, until you grow happy in him. Amen.

"DR. MARTINUS LUTHER.

"*The last day of April, 1531.*"

Weller, the brother of this sorely-tempted woman, was also strongly disposed to melancholy. What Luther had experienced in the monastery, he experienced in Luther's house. He tortured himself, not with definite, grievous sins, but with a false and exaggerated sense of sin. The Reformer, who had already twice given him earnest warning,[*] addressed to him yet further a long and noble epistle in Latin, as follows:[†]

[*] Briefe. De Wette, 4, 39 (June 19, 1530), and 130 (Aug. 10, 1530).
[†] Ibid., 4, 186.

"Grace and Peace in Christ. My dearest Jerome. You should believe firmly that this your temptation comes from the devil, and that he vexes you so because you believe on Christ; for you see in what security and happiness he permits the fiercest enemies of the Gospel, such as Eck, Zwingli and others, to live. We must have the devil for our adversary and enemy, all of us who are Christians, as Peter says (I. v. 8): 'Your adversary, the devil, goeth about.' My dearest Jerome, you should rejoice over this temptation of the devil, for it is a sure sign that God looks upon you with favor and mercy. You say that the temptation is heavier than you can bear, and you fear that it may so break you down and crush you that you may fall into despair and blasphemy. I understand this wile of the devil. If he is unable to cast his victim to the ground at the first assault of temptation, he attempts by persisting to so weary and weaken him that he may fall and acknowledge himself beaten. Therefore, whenever this temptation meets you, be careful not to be drawn into any disputation with the devil, nor to give way to this fatal thought, which would be nothing less than believing and surrendering to him. You must, then, make an earnest effort to boldly despise these thoughts suggested by the devil. The best and easiest way to overcome the devil in temptations and warfare of this kind is just to despise him. Try it. Vanquish the adversary with ridicule, and then look about for some one with whom you can talk. By all means avoid loneliness; for it is just when you are alone that he sets his snares and catches you. This devil is to be overcome by scorn and contempt, not by resisting and disputing with him. Talk a little nonsense, and make merry with my wife and the others, to get the better of those thoughts of the devil, and be of good cheer, my Jerome. This temptation is more necessary for you than food and drink.

"I will tell you what was my experience when I was just about your age. At first, after I had entered the monastery, I went about sad and gloomy, and could not free myself from this spirit of sadness. I therefore sought counsel of Dr. Staupitz, whom I hold ever in grateful remembrance, confessed to him, and revealed to him what terrible and frightful thoughts I had. He replied: 'You do not know, Martinus, how useful and necessary this temptation is for you. God does not exercise you thus for nothing. You will see that he wants your service to accomplish some great things. And so it has turned out; for I can say without boasting that I have become a great doctor, which, at the time when I was enduring this temptation,

I would never have thought possible. Just so it will no doubt be also with you. You will become a great man. Only see to it that you keep up good courage meanwhile, and bear yourself bravely, fully convinced that such words, especially when they come from such learned and great men, are like oracles and prophecies. I recollect that a man whom I was seeking to comfort upon the loss of his son once said to me: 'Mark my word, Martinus, you will yet become a great man.' I very often think of this. Such utterances have, as I have said, something prophetic and oracular about them.

"Take courage, therefore, and cast these deceptive thoughts utterly away from you. As often as the devil tempts you with such thoughts, begin to talk with some one, crack jokes, make sport, or do something else that will cheer you up a little. One has to joke and play a little now and then, * * * just to spite the devil and put him to scorn, so as not to leave him any room to make a conscience for us out of things that are altogether trifling; otherwise, if we are too much concerned for fear we may commit sin, we shall be overcome. We should always do just the opposite of that which Satan commands us. What a very different thing it is to engage in sportive conversation, or to eat and drink oftener than necessary, if I do it only to scorn and despise the devil, who is attempting to torment me and make sport of me! O, that I might perpetrate some sort of a special sin, just to show my scorn for the devil, so that he might see that I recognize no sin and am conscious of none! We must put the whole Decalogue out of sight and out of mind, it seems to me, when the devil thus assaults and vexes us. When the devil casts up to us our sin, and declares us worthy of death and hell, we must say: 'I confess that I am worthy of death and hell. What more have you to say?' 'Then you will be lost forever!' 'Not in the least: for I know One who suffered for me and made satisfaction for my sins, and his name is Jesus Christ, the Son of God. So long as he shall live, I shall live also.'

"THY MARTIN LUTHER.*

"*Nov. 6, 1530.*"

A certain woman, who had suffered an evil word to fall from her lips, was filled in consequence with most distressing thoughts. Luther thus strengthens her:†

"Grace and Peace in the Lord. My dear Lady

---

* A few clauses in the above letter are omitted, as liable to misconstruction in our day.

† Briefe. De Wette, 5, 529. Probably an Eschat, at Herzberg. Ibid., 6, 494.

Margarita. Your brother John informs me, that the evil spirit is burdening your heart, because such an evil word fell from your lips. I wish that the devil might take all those who have * * * * Therefore he vexes you and makes you believe that you shall be his forever.

"Aye, my dear Margarita, since you feel and confess, that it was the evil spirit who led you to utter that evil word, and that it was also his evil suggestion, you ought to remember that everything which he suggests is false; for he is a liar and the father of lies (John viii. 44). It is certainly not Christ who would make you believe that you are to belong to the devil, since he died in order that all who are under the devil's power might be set free from him. Therefore treat the devil thus: Spit on him, and say: 'Have I sinned? Well, then, I have sinned, and I am sorry; but I will not on that account despair, for Christ has borne and taken away all my sin, yes, and the sin of the whole world, if it will only confess its sin, reform and believe on Christ, who has commanded, Luke xxiv. 47, "that repentance and forgiveness of sins be preached in his name among all nations." What should I do if I had committed murder or adultery, or even crucified Christ? Why, even then, I should be forgiven, as he prayed on the cross: "Father, forgive them" (Luke xxiii. 34). This I am in duty bound to believe. I have been acquitted. Then away with you, devil!'

"You ought therefore, dear Margarita, not to believe your own thoughts nor those of the devil, but you should believe us preachers, whom God has commanded to instruct souls, comfort them, and declare them free, as he says (Matt. xvi. 19, John xx. 23): 'Whatsoever ye loose, shall be loosed.' This you ought to believe, and have no doubt at all about it. Now we preachers, in Christ's name and by his command, declare you loosed and free, not only from this one sin, but from all sins which you have inherited from Adam, which are so great and so many that God in mercy will not allow us in this life to see or rightly feel them all, for we could not endure it; much less will he impute them to us who believe on him.

"Be contented, therefore, and of good cheer; your sins are forgiven you. Depend boldly upon this; turn not to your own thoughts, but listen only to that which your pastors and preachers repeat to you out of God's Word. Do not despise their word and comfort; for it is Christ himself who speaks to you through them, as he says, Luke x. 16: 'He that heareth you, heareth me.' Believe this, and the devil will depart and cease troubling you. But if you are still weak in faith, say to yourself: 'I wish that I could believe more firmly, for I know very well that this is true and that it ought to be believed. But even though I cannot believe it as I should, yet I know that it is the pure truth.' That is believing to righteousness and salvation, as Christ says (Matt. v. 6): 'Blessed are they who hunger and thirst after righteousness.'

"May Christ, the dear Lord, who was delivered for our offences and raised again for our justification (Rom. iv. 25), comfort and strengthen your heart in true faith. So far as sins are concerned, you need nothing.

"DR. MARTINUS LUTHER.
"*Thursday after Epiphany (Jany. 11), 1543.*"

The following epistle was written to strengthen in a time of temptation his very dear friend, George Spalatin, who reproached himself most bitterly for his decision in a case of marriage:*

"Grace and Peace from the Lord, and Comfort of the Holy Ghost. Amen. I have heartfelt sympathy for you, my dearest Spalatin, and I pray the Lord to make you strong and cheerful. When I inquired from what sickness you are suffering, I received the

---

* Briefe. De Wette, 5, 679.

reply, that some think you are oppressed with a spirit of melancholy on account of that case of a pastor who married the step-mother of his deceased wife. If that is the trouble, I beseech you by the Lord Christ, as earnestly as I can, not to depend upon yourself and your own thoughts, but to hear the brother in Christ who now speaks to you. Otherwise, the sorrow which, as Paul says, 'worketh death' (2 Cor. vii. 10) will kill you, as I have often learned in my own experience and have also seen in the case of Magister Philip (Melanchthon) at Weimar in 1540, whom sorrow over the case of the Landgrave had already killed, but whom Christ raised up again from the dead in answer to my prayer.

"Granted now, that you are guilty, and that you have sinned in this case; or that you have done a wrong greater and more grievous than that of Manasseh, although the offences which he introduced could not be remedied during all the time following until the destruction of Jerusalem, whereas your offence may be easily remedied, and is only temporal,— granted, I say, that you are guilty: shall sorrow on account of this kill you, and will you, by killing yourself, sin yet far more? It is enough to have sinned; let the sin now vanish, and let sadness, which is a much greater sinner, depart. 'I desire not,' says he (Ezek. xxxiii. 11), 'the death of the sinner, but rather that he may turn from his wickedness and live.' Shall then for you alone the hand of the Lord be too short? Will he in your case have no compassion nor mercy? Will you alone, by means of your sin, rob us of our high-priest, who has compassion upon our weakness? Do you think, then, that it is something wonderful and new, that one who lives in the flesh and is threatened on every hand with so many fiery darts of the devil should for once be wounded, or even thrown to the earth? You seem to me to be without experience in the conflict with sin, conscience and the law. Or, has Satan snatched away from before your eyes and out of your memory all those passages of Scripture in which you have been instructed concerning the office and work of Christ; yes, and all the splendid sermons by which, with such great confidence and exultation of spirit, you have taught, admonished and comforted the church? Or, have you been hitherto such a tender sinner, as to have been troubled only about trifling sins? But, I beseech you, associate yourself with us, the real, great and hard sinners, in order that you may not for us diminish and belittle Christ, who is a Saviour, not of cultivated and slight sinners, but of real sinners, the great as well as the small, yea verily, of all sinners. Thus my Staupitz once comforted me in my sadness. Said he, 'You want to be an imaginary sinner, and to regard Christ as an imaginary Saviour. You must accustom yourself to think that Christ is a real Saviour, and that you are a real sinner. God does nothing for fun nor for show, and he is not joking when he sends his Son and delivers him up for us!'

"If Satan has torn all this and the like out of your memory, so that you cannot of yourself recall it, then just give attention, and hear what I, your brother, have to say, as, standing beyond the reach of your sorrow and unaffected by it, I call upon you, my weak brother, pursued and terrified by Satan, to lean upon me and lift yourself up upon me, until you also, standing erect again, can scorn the devil and sing: 'I have been smitten and shattered, so that I fell, but the Lord helpeth me' (Ps. cxviii. 13). Imagine that I am St. Peter, holding out his hand to you, and saying: 'In the name of Jesus rise up and walk' (Acts iii. 6).

"Hear then, my Spalatin, and believe what Christ says to you through me. I know that I am not mistaken, nor do I speak by instigation of the devil. Christ speaks through me, and commands you to believe your brother who with you believes upon him. He himself declares you free from this sin and from all sins. We have therefore part in your sins, and bear them with you. See to it that you have part with us in the comfort, certain and true, which God himself has commanded us to give to you and has commanded you to receive, since, as we do not wish you to be tormented with sorrow, much less does he desire it. Do not, I pray you, reject him who commands and comforts, and who hates and condemns your sadness, which is an infliction of the devil. Do not permit the devil to represent Christ to you as other than he really is. Your sadness is the devil's work, which Christ will banish, if you will let him. You have been bruised enough; you have suffered enough; you have made atonement enough, yes, far more than enough.

"Remember, my Spalatin, how faithful is the heart of him who ventures thus to speak to you. Believe me, you will thank me best, if you will acknowledge that this my word of comfort is the forgiveness, the absolution, the re-awakening of the Lord himself. If you will acknowledge this, you will find—some day at least—that you have brought to the Lord the most acceptable offering, as is written (Ps. cxlvii. 11): 'The Lord hath pleasure in them that fear him, in those that hope in his mercy.' Away, then, with the sorrow of the devil, who in thee smites us so hard, and attempts to rob us of our joy, and vanquish us all, if possible, at one stroke. But Christ rebukes and will rebuke him. May he also strengthen and preserve you by his Spirit. Amen. Comfort your wife also with these and with better words. I cannot write a second letter now, as time fails me.

"THY MARTIN LUTHER.

"*Zeitz, August 21, 1544.*"

CHAPTER VII.

HOW LUTHER DEALT WITH THE DYING.

IN his comments upon Isa. xxxviii. 10, Luther expresses his views briefly and concisely as to the proper method of preparing for a happy death, in the following words:*

"Thus the monks have written much about preparation for death, but it all amounted to this, that one should forsake the world, *i. e.*, go into a desert or monastery, and there give himself to I know not what manner of meditations. But that is all sheer nonsense. The true preparation for death is the exercise of faith, that one may know that death, sin, hell and Satan are overcome and totally vanquished through Christ, the Crucified; or, in other words, that we regard death, not as it is in and of itself, nor as it appears to us, but as it is in Christ. This looking upon the brazen serpent will preserve us; and there can be no other hope whatsoever, nor any other way to be saved, but to look upon Christ, the Conqueror, in whom death is trodden to the earth, sin overcome, and Satan trampled under

* Werke. Walch, 6, 736.

foot. Upon his Cross hang the trophies of our conquered enemies and tyrants. Thus the heart can in security face death, and feel no terror at sight of the grim spectre."

To regard death otherwise, out of Christ, and to struggle with it, is like swimming in the midst of the sea. Climb up rather into the ship, and cling to the mast, upon which the trophies have been hung. Look neither upon yourself nor upon your own merits, or you will be drowned. But go away from yourself, and draw near to Christ, who is the Lamb of God, the sacrifice for our sins, who took all our sins upon himself and overcame them in his own body, in which the devil and death are crucified. This is the only way to despise death. Although some seek to comfort the dying with the thought, that death will bring all the troubles and dangers of this life to an end, the consolation which they thus offer is weak and cannot support the heart in the struggle. For the dying will suspect that there may be yet greater evils to come after death.

Men must be directed to the sacrifice and the merits of Jesus Christ, our Lord and Deliverer, and Luther rejoices that in the Roman Catholic church this had not been altogether neglected in the last hour, in the final death-struggle. In his brief explanation of the Epistle to the Galatians, he observes under the second verse of the fifth chapter:* "I am very well pleased with the custom of proclaiming before the dying and impressing upon them only Christ, the Crucified, and exhorting them to faith and hope. Here alone, however much the soul-destroying Sophists may have deluded us through our whole life-time, free-will disappears, good works disappear, the righteousness of the law disappears, and there remain only faith and appeal to the pure mercy of God, so that I have often thought that there are more and better Christians in death than in life. The freer the confidence is from good works, and the more entirely it rests upon Christ alone, the better is the Christian; and to this faith all the good works of the whole life are to be attributed. But now we are by so many fogs, clouds and whirlwinds of human traditions and ordinances, as those of the ignorant interpreters of Scripture and preachers, driven in upon our own merits; we of ourselves render satisfaction enough for our own sins; we do not direct our efforts to the laying aside of the frailties of the flesh and bringing to nought the body of sin, but, as though we were already pure and holy, we heap up together a mass of good

* Op. ex. ad Gal. III. 368. Walch., 9, 265.

works, just as men gather wheat into the barn, and by these we are making God our debtor, and will sit on I know not what lofty thrones in Heaven! Blind, blind, blind! Christ is of no account to all these people. They are making themselves righteous in another way."

How Luther himself prepared the dying for a blessed departure from this mortal life, may be seen from two letters. His faithful, thankful heart was moved with pity when he heard that the pilgrimage of his dear father was drawing to a close. He could not hasten to Mansfeld, to bring counsel and help to his dying parent, but was compelled to content himself with the writing of a letter. It reads as follows:*

"To my dear Father, Hans Luther, Citizen of Mansfeld Valley. Grace and Peace in Christ Jesus, our Lord and Saviour. Amen.

"Dear Father: My brother Jacob has written to me that you are thought to be dangerously sick. Since the air is now unhealthy and other dangers abound, as well as on account of your increasing years, I feel much concern for you. God has given and hitherto preserved to you a sound and vigorous body, but yet your age causes me anxiety in these times, although indeed none of us is, or can be,

* Briefe. De Wette, 3, 550.

under any circumstances sure of life for a single hour. I would most gladly therefore come myself to see you in person, but my good friends here have counseled against it and persuaded me not to undertake the journey, and I cannot but think myself that I ought not to tempt God by venturing into danger, for you know what kindly feelings the lords and peasants have for me.

"But it would give me great delight, if it were possible for you and mother to have some one drive you here to us, which my Katie also with tears desires, as do we all. I am sure we would take the best care of you. I have therefore arranged for Cyriacus* to go to you and see whether in your weakness this will be possible. For, whether it should be helpful to you for this life or for that which is to come, as the will of God should ordain, I would be most heartily glad to be with you in body, as is also proper, and, as the fourth commandment teaches, by filial fidelity and service to prove myself thankful to God and to you.

"Meanwhile, I pray from the very depths of my heart to the Father, who created you and gave you to me as a father, that he may according to his in-

---

* This Cyriacus, mentioned already upon page 22, was a son of Luther's sister, who married a certain George Kauffman at Mansfeld. Comp. Briefe. De Wette, 6, 123 and 151.

finite goodness strengthen you, enlighten you by his Spirit and preserve you, that you may with joy and thankfulness know the blessed doctrine of his Son, our Lord Jesus Christ, to which you have already been called and led by his grace out of the former horrible darkness and error; and I hope that his grace, which has given you such knowledge and thereby begun his work in you, may preserve it until the end unto the joyous coming of our Lord Jesus Christ, and complete it in the life which is to come. Amen.

"He has already also sealed in you this doctrine and faith, and confirmed them by visible tokens, inasmuch as you have on account of my name endured, together with us, all much slander, shame, scorn, mockery, contempt, hatred, enmity and danger. But these are the genuine marks, in bearing which we are to be made like our Lord Christ, as St. Paul says (Rom. viii. 29), in order that we may also bear the image of his future glory.

"Let your heart therefore be hale and strong in the midst of your weakness, for we have in the life yonder before God a sure and faithful helper, Jesus Christ, who for us has slain death, together with all sins, and now, in order that we may have no care nor fear that we may sink and perish, sits there upon his throne, and with all the angels looks down upon us, waiting to receive us when we take our departure from this life. He has so great power over death and sin that they can do us no harm; and he is so sincerely true and faithful, that he neither can nor will forsake us, if we really desire his aid.

"He has declared, promised and pledged it. He will not and cannot lie nor deceive us. We can have no doubt about it. 'Ask,' says he (Matt. vii. 7), 'and ye shall receive; seek and ye shall find; knock and it shall be opened unto you.' In another place he declares (Acts ii. 21): 'All that call upon the name of the Lord shall be saved'; and the whole Psalter is full of such consoling promises, especially the 91st Psalm, which is a particularly good Psalm for all the sick to read.

"I have wanted to write these things to you, because I have felt anxious about your sickness, as we do not know when our hour may come, in order that I might have a share in your faith, your conflict, your comfort, and your thankfulness to God for his Holy Word, which he has in these times so richly, powerfully and graciously given to us.

"But should it be his divine will that you, deprived yet longer of the blessedness of that better life, should suffer further with us in this troubled and unhappy world of woe, seeing and hearing, or, rather, with all Christians helping to bear and overcome its misery; he will give you grace to accept all this with cheerful obedience. This accursed life is after all nothing but a real vale of tears, in which the longer we live the more must we see and experience of sin, wickedness, vexation and misfortune; and all this will never end nor grow less until the ground is shoveled upon us. There, at least, it must end, and suffer us, resting in Christ, to sleep in peace until he shall come to awaken us again with rejoicing. Amen.

"Herewith I commend you to him who loves you more than you can love yourself, and who has proved this love in that he has taken your sin upon himself and atoned for it with his own blood, and has announced this to you through the gospel, and through his Spirit granted you grace to believe it, and has thus most securely prepared and sealed everything, in order that you need have nothing more to care for nor to fear, but only with a firm and fearless heart remain steadfast in his Word and faith. Let this be so, then leave all care to him. He will do all things well; yea, he has already done all things for the very best, far better than we can understand. May he, our dear Lord and Saviour, be ever with you, that we may (God grant it, whether here or in the world to come) with rejoicing see one another again. Our faith is firm, and we have no doubt that we shall shortly see one another again in the presence of Christ, since the departure from this life is in the sight of God a much smaller matter than it would be for me to come from your house at Mansfeld to this place, or for you to go from my house at Wittenberg to Mansfeld. This is most certainly true. It is only a matter of an hour's sleep, and then all will be changed.

"Now, although I hope that your pastors and preachers will so abundantly render you in such matters their most faithful service that you will have little need of my poor talking; yet I could not neglect to apologize for my bodily absence, which—God knows—gives me heartfelt pain.

"My Katie, Little Hans, Little Lena, Aunt Lena and the whole household send greetings and assure you of their faithful prayers for you. Greet for me my dear mother and all our relatives. May the grace and power of God be and abide with you forever. Amen.

"Your dear Son,
"MARTINUS LUTHER.
"*At Wittenberg, February 15, 1530.*"

The dying father derived spiritual strength from the letter of his son. His life ebbed slowly away, and on the 29th of May in the same year he fell asleep in the Lord.

"When now," it is related in the Tischreden,* "Michael Coelius, pastor at Mansfeld, asked him at the last moment whether he believed everything which is taught and commended to us in the articles of the Christian Creed, he replied: 'He would be indeed a miserable fellow who would not believe that.' When this was afterwards reported to Dr. Luther, the latter said: 'That is a word from the old world.' But Philip Melanchthon then said to Dr. Luther: 'My dear Doctor, blessed are they who die thus in the knowledge of Christ!'"

One year after his father's death, Luther's mother, Margaretha, was overcome with great weakness. It was seen that her end was near, and word was sent to her distant son. A letter, full of consolation appropriate to the dying hour, was his response.†

"Grace and Peace in Christ Jesus, our Lord and Saviour. Amen. My dearly beloved Mother. I have received the letter of brother Jacob telling of your sickness. It grieves me deeply to hear of this, especially as I cannot be with you in body, as I so gladly would. But here I come to you bodily in this letter, and we will all be constantly with you in spirit.

* Aurif., 500 b. Först., 4, 276.
† Briefe. De Wette, 4, 257.

"But although I hope that your heart has without my help long since been fully instructed, and although, God be praised, you have his consoling Word, and are well provided with preachers and comforters on every hand; yet will I also do my part, and, as in duty bound, acknowledge myself as your child and you as my mother, honoring the relation in which the God and Creator of us both has placed us, and thus, at the same time, adding one more to the multitude of your comforters.

"In the first place, dear Mother, God has graciously given you the knowledge that your sickness is only his paternal and gracious rod, and a very light rod indeed compared with that with which he smites the ungodly, and often, as well, his own dear children. One is beheaded, another banished, another drowned, and so on, until they must all cry out: 'For thy sake are we killed every day, and are like sheep prepared for the slaughter.' (Ps. xliv. 22.) This sickness ought not therefore to disturb nor to distress you, but you ought to accept it with thankfulness as appointed by his grace. Consider what a very trifling affliction it is, should it even lead to death, compared with the suffering of his own dear Son, our Lord Jesus Christ, which he did not have to endure, as must we, for himself, but which he endured for us and for our sins.

"In the second place, dear Mother, you know, too, what is the chief article of faith and the ground of salvation, upon which you must build up your comfort in this and in every hour of need, namely, the Corner-stone, Jesus Christ, that can never be moved nor fail us, nor ever let us sink or perish. He is truly, as he is called, the Saviour of all poor sinners, and of all who in the midst of distress and death place their confidence in him and call upon his name.

"He says (John xvi. 33): 'Be of good cheer; I have overcome the world.' If he has overcome the world, then he has also most assuredly overcome the prince of the world and all his power. But what is the power of the prince of the world, if it be not death, by which he has made us subject to him and taken us captive on account of our sin? But, now that death and sin have been overcome, we may hear with joy and confidence the sweet word: 'Be of good cheer; I have overcome the world.'

"We should have no doubt at all, but should believe that this is most certainly true; and it is still further commanded that we receive this comfort with joy and thanksgiving. If we should refuse to be comforted by these words, we would wrong and greatly dishonor the dear Comforter, just as though it were not true, that he bids us be of good cheer, or as though it were not true, that he has overcome the world. We would thereby strengthen the conquered devil, sin and death, to resist the dear Saviour and tyrannize again over us. From this may God preserve us.

"We may, therefore, now rejoice with all security and joy, and if at any time any thought of sin or death should terrify us, we may lift up our hearts, and boldly say: 'Why, poor Soul, what are you trying to do? Why, Sin and Death, how comes it that you are alive and terrifying me? Do you not know that you have been overcome? Do you not know, O Death, that you are altogether dead? Are you not acquainted with One who says of thee: "I have overcome the world?" It is not for me to listen to your threatenings, but to receive the consoling words of my Saviour: "Be of good cheer, be of good cheer, I have overcome the world." This is the true conquering hero, who bestows upon me his victory and makes me a partaker of it in these words: "Be of good cheer." I hold to him. I am supported by his Word and consolation. Whether I tarry here or depart hence, he will not deceive me. You seek to delude me with your false threatenings and with lying thoughts to entice me away from this victorious Saviour. But it is all a lying invention, as truly as he has overcome you and bidden us to be of good cheer.

'Thus, likewise, Paul also glories and defies the terrors of death (1 Cor. xv. 55): "Death is swallowed up in victory. O Death, where is thy sting? O Grave, where is thy victory?" Thou canst terrify and alarm, like a wooden image of death, but thou hast no power to slay. Thy victory, thy sting, and thy power are swallowed up in the victory of Christ. Thou canst show thy teeth, but thou canst not devour. God has given us the victory over thee through Jesus Christ, our Lord. To him be praise and thanksgiving. Amen.'

"Let your heart be occupied with such words and thoughts, dear Mother, and with nothing else. Be thankful indeed that God has led you to such knowledge, and has not left you sunken in the papal error, according to which we were taught to build our hopes upon our own works and upon the holiness of the monks, and to regard this one and only comfort, our Saviour, not as a comforter, but as a terrible judge and tyrant, so that we were compelled to flee from him to Mary and the saints, and could expect no grace nor comfort from him.

"But now we know, upon the contrary, of the infinite goodness and mercy of our Heavenly

Father, and that Jesus Christ is our Mediator and our Throne of Grace and our Bishop before God in Heaven, who daily intercedes in our behalf and reconciles to God all who will but believe on him and call upon him; and that he is a judge, and terrible, to none but those who will not believe him nor accept his consolation and his grace. He is not the one who accuses or threatens us, but he reconciles and intercedes for us by his own death and by his blood shed for us, that we may not be afraid of him, but draw near to him with all confidence and call him: 'Dear Saviour, Thou precious Comforter, Thou faithful Bishop of our souls.'

"To this knowledge, I say, God has graciously called you—you have his seal and certificate of this, namely, Baptism, the Sacrament, and the Gospel which is preached to you. You can therefore know no danger nor want. Now, only be of good cheer, and give thanks with rejoicing for this great grace; for he who has begun his work in you will also graciously complete it. We cannot help ourselves in such matters. We can by our works gain no booty from sin, death and the devil. But here appears for us and in our place another, who is better able, and he bestows his victory upon us and commands us to accept it, nothing doubting. He says to us (John xvi. 33): 'Be of good cheer; I have overcome the world,' and again (John xiv. 19): 'Because I live, ye shall live also,' and yet again (John xvi. 22): 'Your joy shall no one take from you.'

"May the Father and God of all comfort grant you through his holy Word and his Spirit a steadfast, joyous and thankful faith, that you may happily overcome this and every distress, and finally learn from your own experience the truth of that which he himself declares: 'Be of good cheer; I have overcome the world.' I hereby commend your body and soul to his mercy. Amen. All your children and my Katie are praying for you. Some are weeping, some eating, and they say to one another, 'Grandmother is very sick.' The grace of God be with us all. Amen.

"Your dear Son,
"MART. LUTHER.
"*Saturday after Ascension Day (May 20), 1531.*"

The earthly labors of the mother thus prepared for death by her son were brought to a blessed end on the 30th of June in the same year.

We have seen that Luther gave to his dying father and mother the assurance of his faithful prayer in their behalf. We are able to present several such prayers, dictated by him to the dying, in order that they might by their use strengthen and prepare themselves to depart in peace to their heavenly home.

"Christ, our dear Lord and Saviour," implored he at one time,* "Be gracious to us, that we may not fall into temptation. Preserve us in true faith, pure, blameless and innocent, and deliver us from all evil through a blessed departure from this vale of tears, which is the kingdom of the miserable devil and his world. To Thee, with the Father and the Holy Spirit, be praise and thanksgiving forever. Amen."

At another time, he prayed:† "Dear Lord Christ, although I do not fulfil the law, and although sin is yet present with me, and I fear death and hell, yet I know from thy gospel that Thou hast bestowed upon me all thy works. I am sure of this, for Thou dost not lie. Thou wilt faithfully keep thy promise, in token of which I have received baptism in thy name. Since Thou, O God, art mine, I will gladly die; for thus it pleaseth Thee, my Father, and death cannot harm me, since it is swallowed up in victory. Thanks be to Thee, O Lord God, who hast given us the victory through our Lord Jesus Christ."

* Werke. Walch, 14, 327.
† Ibid., 21, 287.

Upon a third similar occasion, he spoke thus:* "Almighty, eternal God, merciful Lord and God, who art the Father of our dear Lord Jesus Christ, I know assuredly that Thou wilt and canst do all that Thou hast promised, for Thou canst not lie and thy Word is sure. Thou didst in the beginning promise to me thy beloved, only Son Jesus Christ, and he has come and has delivered me from the devil, death, hell and sin, and then, for my greater security, of his gracious will granted me the sacraments of the altar and of baptism, in which are offered to me the forgiveness of sins, eternal life and all heavenly possessions. In accordance with this thine offer to me, I have employed the sacraments, and have received them, depending in steadfast faith upon thy Word. I have, therefore, now no doubt that I am safe and well secured against the devil, death, hell and sin. If this be my appointed hour, according to thy holy will, I will gladly depart hence in peace and joy, depending on thy Word. Amen."

We will observe the dear man of God as he stands by the death-beds of two persons in his own house. An aunt of his wife, who had years before, in the convent of Nimbsch, treated her younger

---

* Tischreden. Aurif., 501 a. Först., 4, 278. Comp. Aurif., 326 a. Först, 3, 153.

relative with the greatest kindness, had been taken by Luther into his house as a member of the family. She was called "Aunt Lena" by old and young. This "honorable matron" lay seriously sick in 1537. Her senses had already become dull, when the father of the household approached her bed, addressing her thus:* "Aunt Lena, do you know me, and can you understand me?" Seeing that she understood and recognized him, he said to her: "Your faith still rests entirely and alone upon the Lord Christ, does it not? He is the resurrection and the life. Nothing shall keep you from him. You shall not die, but fall asleep as in a cradle, and when the morning dawns, you shall rise again and live forever." Then she exclaimed, "O yes!" The Doctor then asked her: "Is there no trouble on your mind?" "No," replied she. "And do you have no pain at all?" "Yes," said she, "I have a pain at my heart." Then said he: "The Lord will soon deliver you from all evil; you will not die!" and, turning to us, he said: "O, how well it is with her! This is not death, but a sleep!" He then went to the window and stood for a little time alone praying, and at twelve o'clock withdrew from the room. At seven o'clock the same evening she very gently fell asleep in Christ.

*Tischreden. Aurif., 325 b. Först., 3, 153.

A sweet little daughter of Luther's, named Magdalena, after this same Aunt Lena, who had been sick-nurse in the convent from 1502 until 1508, and had turned her experience and skill to good account in her niece's home, lay seriously sick. "I love her dearly, but if it is thy will, O God, to take her from us, I will be glad to know that she is with thee."* Thus the pious father quiets his troubled heart, and then says to his beloved child: "Dear little Magdalena, my daughter, you would gladly stay here with your father, and yet you are glad to go to your Father in Heaven, are you not?" She said: "Yes, my dearly beloved father, as God will." "Then," said the father, "you dear little daughter, the spirit is willing, but the flesh is weak," and, turning away, he said, "O, but I do love her. If the flesh is so strong, what must the spirit be?" "Dear daughter," said he again after a little while,† "you have another Father in Heaven, you are going to him." As the final struggle drew near and she was just at the point of death, "the father fell upon his knees before her bed, wept bitterly, and prayed that God might release her. She died thus, falling asleep in her father's arms. Her mother was also in the

---

* Tischreden. Aurif., 496 a. Först., 4, 260.

† Ibid. Aurif., 496 a. Först., 4, 261.

same room, but standing farther from the bed, overcome with grief. This occurred a little after nine o'clock on the Wednesday following the 17th Sunday after Trinity (Sept. 20), 1542." Observing that his wife was now overwhelmed with grief, weeping and crying, Luther said to her: "Dear Katie, remember whither she has gone! She has gone to a better world! It is but natural that flesh and blood should bleed and groan; but the spirit bows submissively. Children do not dispute. They believe what is said to them. To them everything is plain and simple. They die without anxiety or regret, without murmuring, without any fear of death, without bodily pain, just as though they were falling asleep."* When the friends came to assist in preparing the body for burial, and addressed the Doctor in the customary way, assuring him that they sympathized with him in his affliction, he said: "You ought to rejoice with me! I have sent a saint to Heaven, yes, a living saint. O, that we might have such a death! Such a death I would welcome this very hour."†

* Tischreden. Aurif., 495 b. Först. 4, 258.
† Ibid. Aurif., 496 b. Först., 4, 262.

www.ingramcontent.com/pod-product-compliance
Lightning Source LLC
Chambersburg PA
CBHW022007220426
43663CB00007B/990